KT-458-925

SAMUEL HAHNEMANN

A completely fresh biography of Samuel Hahnemann, the
founder of homoeopathy, tracing his wandering life through
persecution and tragedy to eventual success and the
establishment of homoeopathic medicine throughout
the world.

Frontispiece. Dr Samuel Hahnemann.

SAMUEL HAHNEMANN

The Founder of Homoeopathic Medicine

by

TREVOR M. COOK

M.Sc., Ph.D., C.Eng., M.I.Prod.E., C.Chem., F.R.S.C.

THORSONS PUBLISHERS LIMITED
Wellingborough, Northamptonshire

First published in 1981

© TREVOR M. COOK 1981

PA. **650381**

8\88

HAH

This book is sold subject to the condition that it shall not, by way of trade or otherwise, be lent, re-sold, hired out, or otherwise circulated without the publisher's prior consent in any form of binding or cover other than that in which it is published and without a similar condition including this condition being imposed on the subsequent purchaser.

British Library Cataloguing in Publication Data

Cook, Trevor M.
  Samuel Hahnemann.
  1. Hahnemann, Samuel
  2. Homeopathic physicians — Biography
  I. Title
  615.5'32'0924   RX66.H2

ISBN 0-7225-0689-9
ISBN 0-7225-0740-2 Pbk

Typeset by Harper Phototypesetters, Northampton.
Printed in Great Britain by
Nene Litho, Earls Barton, Northamptonshire,
and bound by Weatherby Woolnough,
Wellingborough, Northamptonshire.

Dedicated to the memory of my father
Henry A. Cook

CONTENTS

LIST OF ILLUSTRATIONS

PREFACE

During the three years I have spent researching and writing this biography of the founder of homoeopathy, my admiration for Dr Christian Frederick Samuel Hahnemann has remained undiminished. Nevertheless, this is not a eulogy, and I have tried to present him as a man, with all his strengths and human feelings. From what I have come to know of him I believe he would have wished it this way. In addition to references to his medical and scientific work I have, therefore, included material which is relevant to the character, and our understanding of the man himself. In my view, to know Hahnemann is to know homoeopathy.

Apart from his own historic achievements, I have also attempted to weave into the text the other momentous events of his time which influenced Hahnemann's life and work and which were to shape the world's history up to the present day.

I have taken some licence in rephrasing certain documents where the meaning is clearer in the modern idiom, but never to the extent that facts are altered. In writing of the kaleidoscopic events in Hahnemann's life, I have striven to seek the truth, for I was ever mindful of his own expression, 'Machts nach, aber machts recht nach' (Report me, but report me correctly).

I am most indebted to so many people in the preparation of the manuscript, or for their encouragement or helpful comments, and I offer my apologies in advance to those omitted from the following: my family; R. W. Wilson; G. O. Young; J. Crawford; J. C. Pert; Wendy Killick; Hilda Jackson; Lt. Col. M. C. Barraclough; Dr June Burger; Forrest Murphy; Dr Frederic Schmid; the Librarian of the Pharmaceutical Society; the Burgomeister of Meissen and the City Archives Department; the

National Center of Homeopathy, U.S.A.; the American Institute of Homeopathy; the Hahnemann Society. I would like to thank them all most sincerely.

The water colour of Hahnemann's house in Meissen and the portrait of Dr Frederick Hervey Foster Quin are reproduced by the kind permission of The Hahnemann Trust. The portrait of Queen Adelaide is reproduced by the kind permission of The National Portrait Gallery.

Please note that, unless stated otherwise, the quotations preceding each chapter are taken from the works of Samuel Hahnemann.

TREVOR M. COOK
London, 1981

PROLOGUE

MUNICIPAL OFFICES OF THE DEPARTMENTS OF THE
SEINE CITY OF PARIS

3 July 1843, 10 a.m.

CERTIFICATE OF DEATH relating to Mr Christian Friedrich
Samuel Hahnemann, physician, 89 years of age, widower by his
first marriage with Johanna Leopoldine Henriette Küchler;
second marriage with Marie Melanie of no profession, 38 years of
age. The above mentioned deceased was born in Meissen (Saxony)
and died in Paris in his own house, No. 1 Rue de Milan, yesterday
at 5 a.m.

In the grey half-light, shortly before five on the morning of 11 July
1843, the hearse drew up in the large courtyard of the imposing
eighteenth century mansion at No. 1 Rue de Milan. It was a sultry
morning and it was raining.

Whilst the bearers were carrying the plain wooden coffin downstairs it lurched awkwardly, and the widow, Mrs Melanie
Hahnemann, remonstrated with the men for fear that the
bannister might be damaged. The coffin was hoisted unceremon-
iously onto the hearse and the driver paused only long enough for
the small party of mourners to assemble behind, before moving
through the iron gates into the Rue de Clichy. Following on foot
were the widow, the deceased's daughter Amalie and her son
Leopold, Dr Le Thiere (a young apothecary) and a few servants of
the household.

As the melancholy cortège turned into the Place de Clichy the
rain increased to a torrent causing the horses' black plumes to wilt

and muffling the clatter of hooves which had echoed along the deserted street. Bearing left from the Boulevard de Clichy and up the short hill, they entered Montmartre Cemetery and, at public grave No. 8, the coffin was deposited in an old, three-tiered brick vault in the uppermost section above two other coffins. The aperture of the upper section was rather small and the bearers were obliged to force in the rain-soaked coffin, causing it some damage.

As the vault was sealed by locking a rusting grilled iron gate in position, leaving the three coffins in view, those in attendance turned away and dispersed in silence. No prayers were said; no hymns were sung; no orations, no speeches; no blessing. Barely thirty minutes had passed since the hearse had arrived at the house.

Yet this was not the end, nor was it the beginning. Rather, it was the end of the beginning. For the dead man, Dr Christian Friedrich Samuel Hahnemann, had established a system of healing which had revolutionized medicine and was already sweeping the world. Even today, more than 170 years later, it is enjoying more support than ever before. In his long, troubled, stormy life, this tragic, obdurate, enigmatic reformer had fought against the corruption and ignorance of a bigoted and reaction-ary medical profession. He had endured obloquy and contempt in seeking a more humane and natural system of treatment than the barbaric practices of that time, when more patients succumbed to their treatment than their disease, to reach a certain tranquillity in his old age amidst continuing controversy, and to earn the gratitude of generations of people yet to come.

1.

EARLY DAYS
(1755-1771)

The highest ideal of cure is the speedy, gentle and enduring
restoration of health by the most trustworthy and least
harmful way.

In the spring of 1755 a second son was born to Christian Gottfried
and Johanna Christian Hahnemann of Meissen in south-east
Germany. He was born shortly before midnight on Thursday, 10
April, and was given the names Christian Friedrich Samuel. To
avoid confusion with his father's first name, the boy became
known simply as Samuel Hahnemann. So close to midnight was
his birth, some doubt remains as to the exact date, for the church
register recorded 11 April. The omission of the second 'h' in
'Hahnemann' in the entry casts some doubt on the accuracy of
the Registrar, but the final arbiter must be Samuel Hahnemann
himself, who celebrated his birthday on 10 April throughout his
lifetime. The infant Samuel was not particularly robust, which
may be inferred from his unusually early christening, recorded in
the same church register as his birth, on 13 April 1755, probably
necessitated by a short life expectancy.

The small, but important town of Meissen in Saxony, of some
four thousand inhabitants at the time of the birth of its most
illustrious son, is now part of East Germany. It is situated about
150 miles south of Berlin on a small hill at the mouth of a broad
fertile valley where the River Elbe and its tributaries, the
Triebisch and the Meisa, rise from the plains in the north
through undulating hills to the Erz Mountains bordering with
Czechoslovakia. Meissen was founded in A.D. 929 by King
Heinrich I, when he had a castle built on the hill.

Although a great fire in 1637 had destroyed a large section of the centre of the town, its castle, spires and many beautiful fifteenth to seventeenth century mansions, viewed across the River Elbe from the east bank, were (and still are today) particularly impressive. From medieval times, the town was the centre of a flourishing cloth trade. Since 1710 the town had had a world reputation for its fine quality porcelain, and for many centuries fine Meissen wine had been produced from the vines cultivated on the sunny slopes of the hills, mainly on the bank of the Elbe upstream from the town.

In the centre of the town, on the west bank of the river, stood the ancient Frauenkirche cathedral, first mentioned in records dated 1205 as a market chapel, with its stone tower and richly guilded carved altar dating from 1500. Nearby, on the brow of the hill, was the world-famous porcelain factory situated in the old Albrecht Castle, built between 1471 and 1483 by Arnold von Westfalen, and now long since deserted by the Dukes of Saxony when they moved further up the valley to more fashionable Dresden. Close by the Frauenkirche stood the *Rathaus*, or Town Hall, built in 1472 in classic Gothic style, and the two buildings formed two sides of the market square. South of the town centre, at the end of Neumarkt, stood the beautiful St Nicolaikirche, founded in the twelfth century, with its choir adorned with Gothic murals. Rosa Hobhouse quoted her husband's impressions when he visited Meissen in 1931.

> The main features of Meissen are still much as they were in Samuel Hahnemann's youthful days, with a picturesque mass of high, gabled roofs crowded along the base and slopes of a long and beautiful valley, one side still wooded and the other dominated by the cathedral and castle.

This was the setting that the infant Samuel was to come to love and to which, throughout his travels during his long life, he would always seek to return. Meissen and Torgau, twenty-five miles to the north (where Samuel Hahnemann lived later), were to feature in another historical event nearly two centuries later, when the advancing Allied armies met the Russian army on the bridges across the Elbe on 25 April 1945, to complete the defeat of

1.　Meissen today.

Nazi Germany in the Second World War.

Samuel's mother, Johanna, married Christian Hahnemann on 2 November 1750 in Kötzchenbroda, a suburb of Dresden, where her father was stationed as a Quartermaster Captain. Her husband had become a widower at 28 when his first wife, Johanne Deerens, whom he married in Meissen in 1748, died nine months after giving birth to twins, one stillborn, the other living only nine months. The house where Samuel was born was purchased for 437 talers (about £175) by his father two years before, in 1753, after Johanna gave birth to Samuel's elder sister, Charlotta Gerharduna. It was a modest, three-storied house, half a mile to the south of the town centre, on the corner of Neumarkt and Fleischsteg, and within a stone's throw of the old St Nicolai-kirche, the building itself being then known as the *Eckhaus*. It was here that young Samuel would live until he was twenty years old.

Samuel's father, Christian Gottfried Hahnemann, was born in Lauchstadt, a small town about 50 miles north-west of Meissen, near the River Saale, a tributary of the Elbe, on 24 July 1720. He was a sensitive man possessing high principles. He was devoutly religious and believed passionately in the value of discipline, hard work and compliance with the fifth commandment as firmly re-capitulated by Martin Luther. Although his formal education ceased when he was no more than twelve or thirteen years old, he had improved his knowledge through reading and had developed his artistic talent. He was the fifth child of Samuel's grandfather, Christoph (sometimes spelled Christoff) Hahnemann, who was an artist.

Christoph's father, Samuel's great-grandfather, was probably called Christian, and like his son, he was not a native of Lauch-stadt, nor even that part of Saxony. The church registers of Lauchstadt show clearly that Christoph and a Christian Hahnemann (almost certainly his brother) came to live there at about the same time in 1707. Christoph had seven children, all born in Lauchstadt: Christoph (born December 1711), Johanna (born April 1714), Christiana (born May 1716), Theodora (born March 1718), Christian Gottfried (Samuel's father), Christian August (born June 1722) and Dorothea (born October 1724). It is noteworthy that the godparents of all the children were civic

2.   Hahnemann's house in Meissen (a water colour by G. Werner dated 1855).

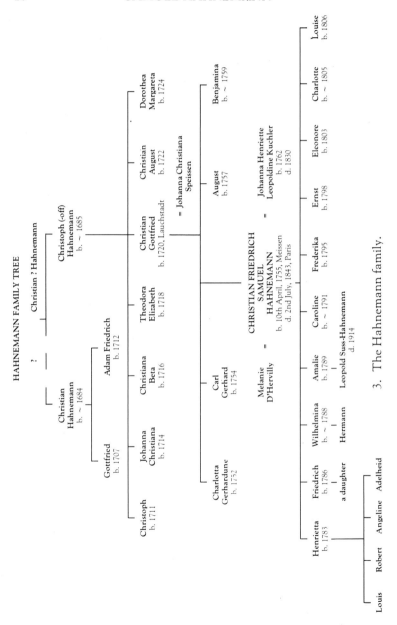

HAHNEMANN FAMILY TREE

Christian ? Hahnemann

?

Christian
Hahnemann
b. ~ 1684

Christoph (-off)
Hahnemann
b. ~ 1685

Adam Friedrich
b. 1712

Gottfried
b. 1707

Johanna
Christiana
b. 1714

Christiana
Beta
b. 1716

Theodora
Elizabeth
b. 1718

Christian
Gottfried
b. 1720, Lauchstadt

Christian
August
b. 1722

Dorothea
Margareta
b. 1724

= Johanna Christiana
Speissen

Christoph
b. 1711

Charlotta
Gerhardune
h. 1752

Carl
Gerhard
b. 1754

CHRISTIAN FRIEDRICH
SAMUEL
HAHNEMANN
b. 10th April, 1755, Meissen
d. 2nd July, 1843, Paris

=

Melanie
D'Hervilly

August
b. 1757

Benjamina
b. ~ 1759

=

Johanna Henriette
Leopoldine Kuchler
b. 1762
d. 1830

Henrietta
b. 1783

Friedrich
b. 1786

a daughter

Wilhelmina
b. ~ 1788

Hermann

Amalie
b. 1789

Leopold Suss-Hahnemann
d. 1914

Caroline
b. ~ 1791

Frederika
b. 1795

Ernst
b. 1798

Eleonore
b. 1803

Charlotte
b. ~ 1805

Louise
b. 1806

Louis   Robert   Angeline   Adelheid

3. The Hahnemann family.

dignitaries, civil servants or merchants, indicating that, at that time at least, the Hahnemann family enjoyed a certain prosperity and social standing in the community. Harder times, through ill fortune and war, were to come.

Samuel's paternal grandfather, his father and his uncle, Christian August, were all artists. All the entries in the church registers in both Lauchstadt and Meissen described their occupations as 'painters', whilst records in the porcelain factory in Meissen, where the brothers were employed, described August, more specifically, as a painter of flowers and landscapes. Although many specimens of Meissen porcelain of this period exist today, it is not possible to attribute any artwork to the Hahnemanns, as it was not the practice, at that time, for work to be signed.

Samuel's brief autobiography records that his father had a small book published on painting in water colours. On his marriage, one of his most treasured wedding gifts was an ivory fan, depicting a family scene and decorated with flowers, painted by his father. Although it was clear from the beginning that young Samuel would not follow in the family tradition, and would develop his aptitude for science and medicine, there is evidence to suggest that he had a certain artistic talent. He would sometimes adorn his letters and student papers with drawings and sketches, and his sense of humour was apparent when he signed his name in the form of an accurate drawing of a cock, with the suffix '-emann' ('Hahn', being the German word for cock). Later in life, his technical drawings confirmed this ability.

Records of Samuel's boyhood are somewhat sparse. He was a thin, physically delicate, fair-haired boy with clear, almost piercing, eyes. He did not enjoy robust health and was of a studious disposition. He was well disciplined, and he showed great respect and affection for his parents, both of whom shared in his education. In his home, like many 'burgher class' homes of the time, high moral standards, solidity, industry, sobriety, frugality, orderliness and piety prevailed under his father's stiff, but kindly eye. Born into the Lutheran Protestant faith, he would accompany his family on Sundays to the services at the Protestant church and, although he retained a religious fervour all his life, like his contemporaries Rousseau and Voltaire, his later religious freethinking was decidedly deistic.

He would walk to the end of Neumarkt and up the Marktgasse to visit the market with his mother, and he explored the river banks and roamed the hills behind the town, accompanied by his elder brother by one year, Carl, his younger brother, August (who was born in 1757 and was later to become a field apothecary in Austria), and his sisters, Charlotta (who was to marry twice, first a pastor and then a civil servant) and the young Benjamina, affectionately called by the diminutive 'Minna' by the family. On rare occasions he visited the old City Theatre (*Theaterplatz*), behind the Town Hall, which had recently been rebuilt after being burnt to the ground by the Swedes in 1637.

Dudgeon (1854) reported that Samuel kept a collection of local plants and flowers. He gives this quote from Hahnemann.

> In my boyhood days I became interested in the study of botany. On my excursions into the neighbouring hills I stopped by the wayside, in inns, to assort and press my plants. Here, when a boy, I heard and learned the popular phrases and expressions of the people. My father, who was very strict, did not allow us to make use of any vulgar expressions. One time when I was walking along the road, I met a farmer who asked me if I knew what the word *Standpunkt* [standpoint] meant; saying that his minister was preaching all the time about 'standpoint', and to him, the farmer, it seemed to be most ridiculous to talk about a thing with no meaning. In the evening I repeated the conversation to my father and several older gentlemen who were present. They all laughed heartily and said it was nonsense to use such unmeaning language, especially when speaking to the illiterate.

Certainly Samuel developed an affinity with, and a deep love for, the countryside and his native Saxony, and it is significant that until the age of eighty, when he left his own country for reasons that will be revealed, his travels never took him far from the course of the River Elbe—from Mölln in the north to Dresden in the south. In his short autobiography he wrote, 'The Electorate of Saxony is one of the most beautiful parts of Germany. This may have contributed to my veneration of the beauties of nature as I grew up to manhood.' Subsequently he recorded, 'The instinctive

longing of a Swiss for his rugged Alps cannot be any more irresistible than that of a Saxon for his native soil.' As Pope wrote,

> Happy the man, whose wish and care,
> A few paternal acres bound,
> Content to breathe his native air,
> In his own ground.

Unfortunately Samuel's boyhood was marred by the hardship,
danger, curfews and restricted travel which affected the whole
community throughout the Seven Years War from 1756 to 1763.
King Frederick II of Prussia, fighting Austria for Silesia, was aided
by a reluctant Britain, under King George II (and later George III)
who was preoccupied with the French threat to the American
colonies. An Anglo-Prussian army was formed, under the
command of Duke Ferdinand of Brunswick, to check the French
invasion of Germany. On entering Saxony, Frederick plundered
all the porcelain and much cloth throughout the Meissen area to
help finance his army, and it took several years for the standard of
living of the porcelain factory workers to recover. For this reason,
Samuel's boyhood was also punctuated by periods of menial work
to supplement the family's income.

Samuel's father and mother, being of limited means, gave him
his early education themselves. Although he had not studied
science, and lacked a broad general education, Christian
Gottfried gave his son a sound grounding, coupled with the
highest standards of behaviour. Again quoting Samuel's autobiography,

> My father found for himself the soundest conceptions of that
> which is good and can be called worthy of man. These ideas he
> implanted in me. To act and live without pretence or show was his
> most noteworthy precept, which impressed me more by his
> example than by his words . . . His ideas on the first principles of
> creation, the dignity of mankind, and its lofty destiny, seemed
> consistent in every way with his mode of life. This was the
> foundation of my moral training.

Haehl (1922) reported that Christian spoke of giving his son
what he called 'thinking lessons'. A Professor Fluegel reported
that, on a visit to Meissen many years later, he was told by one of

the older workers at the porcelain factory that Samuel's father was in the habit of locking up his young son when leaving for the factory, having given him a difficult problem to solve or to think about, until his return.

In February 1762, when only six years old, Samuel suffered the loss of his elder brother, Carl Gerhard, who died at the age of seven years. The cause of death was not recorded. Although at such a tender age, young Samuel's grief was short-lived, as becoming the eldest surviving son of the family was to give him extra responsibilities, not the least of which being the necessity to earn wages to help in support of his family. Inevitably, this interrupted his early education.

Samuel attended the Town Elementary School in Meissen until he was fifteen years old. There were two schools in the town at that time, one being the old Latin Town School, or *Volksschule*, and the other, in which Samuel was later to begin serious study, the Prince's Grammar School. The Town School register carries an entry, dated 20 July 1767:

> Christian Friedrich Samuel Hahnemann, son of the porcelain painter, 12 years old, Class 2.

His attendance at the school was intermittent, however. Samuel's autobiography relates, 'My father repeatedly took me away from the Town School for more than a year at a time, so that I might pursue some business more suited to his income.' Fortunately, in Samuel's later years at the school, his teachers, having recognized his exceptional academic potential, refused to accept any fees and his absences were less frequent.

One teacher in particular, Magister Johann Müller, who taught Samuel Latin, Greek and German, had a particular influence in his studies. Realizing that he was a pupil of exceptional ability, he gave Samuel extra tuition and a preference over other pupils, and a mutual respect and admiration developed between them. At the age of twelve, Samuel was entrusted by Johann Müller to teach younger boys the rudiments of Greek. Samuel himself was to relate later, 'Magister Müller loved me as his own child . . . I owe him a great debt of gratitude for in honesty and diligence few could equal him.' ('Magister' was a title used in Germany to signify a Master of Arts, and later a Doctor of Philosophy.)

These austere, yet happy, formative years in the bosom of his family, were to inculcate young Samuel in the strong moral values and a love of God which were to serve him well in the tortuous, turbulent years to come.

2.

STUDENT DAYS
(1771-1779)

Every medicine which, among the symptoms it can cause in a
healthy body, reproduces those most present in a given disease,
is capable of curing that disease in the swiftest, most thorough
and most enduring fashion.

Samuel Hahnemann had long since decided in his own mind that
he wished to follow a scholastic career, but there were a number of
circumstances, overtly unconnected, which caused this wish to
be realized. The Seven Years War was over, bringing an improvement in his father's financial circumstances, but, as I have said,
the untimely death of his brother had placed extra responsibilities
on his shoulders. With other children to educate, Christian
Hahnemann decided that Samuel should end his studies and,
shortly before his fifteenth birthday, despatched him to work in a
grocery store in Leipzig. A studious philologist, Samuel found the
work intolerable and he became homesick. After much un-
happiness, he left the home of his employer with whom he lived
and, fearful of his father's wrath, he returned to Meissen. Rosa
Hobhouse reported that the young truant was hidden by his
mother for several days until she was sure that he would receive a
sympathetic reception from his father.

About this time Johann Müller, whose protégé Samuel had
become at the Town School, was appointed Rector, or *Tertuis*, at
the Prince's Grammar School. On 17 November 1770, Samuel's
father wrote (in the exaggerated, obsequious style of that time) to
the Archduke of Saxony, Friedrich August, to formally request
that his son be admitted to the Prince's School.

My Gracious Prince and Lord, Serene Highness, Gracious Prince and Master. May herewith my submissive and most obedient petition come before Your Serene Highness, that you will graciously grant, You, who benevolently care for the welfare and education of youth, that my son, Christian Friedrich Samuel Hahnemann, may not only frequent the public lessons at the Prince's School as extraneous, but that he may be also entrusted to the special instruction and supervision of the teacher, Magister Johann August Müller.

That his father had succumbed to the entreaties of Samuel and his mother was clear, but Haehl (1922) suggested that it was Johann Müller who, knowing that he was taking up his new appointment at the school, played a major part in convincing Christian that his son had exceptional academic ability and should not be denied the opportunity to continue his studies.

The Archduke replied to Christian Hahnemann's submissive petition on 21 November, authorizing his son to attend the school, 'desiring herewith that you take obedient notice and make the necessary arrangements for it'. It was thus that Samuel became a pupil of the Prince's Grammar School at Easter, 1771, at about the same time as his tutor, Johann Müller, took up his appointment as Rector.

The Prince's School had been established in 1544 by the then Elector of Saxony to replace the school which existed previously in the disbanded Augustine monastery of St Afra. The old St Afrakirche, built around 1300, still stood behind the school. The school motto read, 'Sapere Aude' ('Dare to be wise'), and these words from the Roman poet and satirist, Horace, were to be used by Samuel many years later on the title page of the later editions of his most important work, The Organon of the Art of Healing. From its monastic origins the school inherited a tradition for strict discipline for which, by virtue of his father's upbringing, Samuel was singularly well prepared. It is noteworthy that the school enjoyed a fine reputation for its academic standards and boasted several exceptional pupils, later to achieve fame. One of these former pupils, Gotthold Lessing (1729-81), wrote his dramatic masterpiece, Miss Sara Sampson, the first tragedy of German common life, in the year Samuel was born, and he was later to influence decisively the course of German literature, as Samuel was to do in medicine. Another former pupil was the poet, Christian Gellert (1715-69); one of his poems was to feature in Samuel's greatest work in the years to come.

In the ensuing four years Samuel was able to develop his talent for languages, mathematics, geometry and botany, guided and encouraged by Herr Müller, with whom he developed a lasting friendship. Twenty years later he wrote, 'He [Müller] accorded me liberties in my studies for which I am thankful to this day, and which exerted a perceptible influence upon my subsequent studies. ... . I had free access to him at any time of day . . . all this put together says much, considering that it was a Prince's School of Saxony.'

Samuel proved to be a most diligent student. Still physically delicate, he was as he himself put it, 'frequently ailing from over-studying'. Many years later he wrote to a student who consulted him, 'Mental exertion and study are unnatural occupations for the young whose bodily development is not yet complete, especially for those with sensitive feelings. This nearly cost me my life during the period [when he was studying at the Prince's School] from fifteen to twenty years of age.'

In his final term—the Spring Term of 1775—Samuel wrote a dissertation in Latin, which was the custom at that time, entitled 'The Wonderful Construction of the Human Hand'. The choice of subject demonstrated his inclination towards a career in the medical profession. A few days before Easter, Samuel read his dissertation at the annual ceremony called the *Schule Entlassungstag* or School Speech Day, held in the Assembly Hall. He was called onto the platform, where his teachers were assembled, and facing an audience of civic dignitaries in their full regalia, past pupils and proud parents, including his own mother and father, he delivered his oration in Latin, with a firm and solemn voice. We are indebted to Stephen Hobhouse for tracing a copy of Samuel's dissertation. It began:

> No one among you, most learned and illustrious auditors, can doubt that it may be known and understood from the mechanism of the whole universe that God exists; and yet I think that I may with truth assert that it is above all else in the construction of the

human body that the wonderful wisdom and beneficence of the Supreme Being is most radiantly clear. For in each and every limb He has shown such incredible skill of craftsmanship and such exquisite art, that anyone who dares to cast blame on the least thing in the composition of our bodies may rightly and deservedly be considered not merely foolish, but devoid of all sense and insight. Moreover, as man is easily the chief of all living creatures, so the dignity and excellence of his body far exceeds that of theirs.

What I have just said is indeed obvious to every careful observer. And yet the perfection of skill which is also shown in the build of the other animals will be readily regarded as most worthy of admiration by anyone who grasps how aptly and fittingly their various senses and limbs have been planned and created by the Supreme Maker of the world, so as to suit the diversity of character and strength in each creature. The horse is endowed with solid hoofs and a handsome mane, for he is a swift and proud animal. While the lion, a brave and ferocious beast, has been supplied by the same wise and divine Nature with powerful teeth and claws. For a similar reason the bull and the wild boar have powers of defence and natural ornaments corresponding to the character of each. As for timid species like the deer and the hare, what gifts more fitting could there be than their marvellous agility of limb and their speed of foot, in so much as they are without any direct protection against violence?

But for man, who has the divine gift of a mind, hands have been created by Nature as the sole instruments of defence—hands which are adapted for his use and guardians of his safety. Man accordingly had no need of the natural endowment of horns and claws, since the tips of his fingers were provided with nails and he could use sword and spear and other kinds of weapons, some of them sharper and some harder than horns. I need hardly, add that, even from a distance, he is able to repel attacks and wound another creature, with a stone, for example, or a club, or those iron tubes which project leaden bullets, and with other similar weapons; while beasts, unlike man, can only fight and protect themselves at close quarters. All these actions are within our power with the help of the hands.

What shall I say of the arts discovered with the aid of the hands? Or of the clothing manufactured by them? What of the buildings constructed for our comfort and for usefulness and protection? Moreover, what laws would we possess, what records of genius, if we were without hands? The hands are assuredly the benefactors that enable us to hold converse with Plato and with Aristotle, with Hippocrates and with Galen, and with other luminaries of the ancient world. I am convinced that everyone will agree with me, that for a creature endowed with wisdom, there is nothing of greater use and benefit than a pair of hands.

But so that I may myself lay before you the truths that I have gathered from a rapid survey of the scientific writers in the course of my leisure studies, as they are called, I would beg your leave now, my most honoured auditors, to set forth briefly to you what a skilful work of the Divine Wisdom and Providence is to be found in the human hands. Now, to begin with, the hand seems to have been shaped and constructed precisely with the object of being able·to take the place of the various tools for which there is any place in life, for example of the hammer, the hook and the pincers. For what craftsman other than the Creator of the universe, who has infinite wisdom and foresight, could have secured such a capacity for skill as there is in the hands? For he has given us hands which are so divided and parted into fingers that they are able to hold and clasp round anything of a spherical shape, and also, by extending all the fingers, to grasp even rather large objects, and smaller ones by the pressure of two fingers only. And so in general they can adjust themselves easily to any shape. . . . [he then described the anatomical details of the human hand] . . . And now, my most esteemed auditors, I will pass over, for fear of seeming tedious to you, any description of the dexterous contrivance by which the tendons and sinews are closely connected with and hung from the muscle of the arms, and thus control and guide each of the finger joints. I will pass over the capacity of the fingers for incredibly rapid motion, their power in grasping, the ease with which they may be contracted and extended, the speed with which they may be directed sideways, the strength of the thumb, and finally the admirable character of the muscles. For the whole subject is such a source of wonder and delight that it seems preferable to omit it altogether than to speak of it too briefly.

Let me therefore, honoured and learned auditors, conclude at length by saying that I hold myself to have briefly proved to you, as far as the weakness of my poor capacities has permitted me, that the mechanism of our hands has been elaborated and brought to perfection by the Allwise Creator of the world with a marvellous and divine craftmanship. And you, finally, my good comrades in school, let me admonish and beseech you to venerate with me that

Supreme Providence which has assuredly given a clear revelation of itself as much in the least of created beings as in the wisest and mightiest of the angels. For believe me, He has equipped and adorned our minds with understanding and intelligence for no other reason, save that we may gain a knowledge of Himself—a knowledge which we may have by contemplating ourselves and other things that He has created; and this wonderful sight is not possible to any other species of living creatures.

After delivering his oration, Samuel expressed his gratitude for the help and support he had received in his studies from Magister Müller and his other teachers, his parents and family. He did this in the form of a poem—this time written in French—a further demonstration of his gift for languages. The well-deserved applause he received, as he left the platform to rejoin his parents in the audience, marked the end of his secondary education.

The Mayor of Meissen has kindly provided the author with details of the modern city in 1980. The Prince's School, or *Fursten und Landesschule*, existed until 1941. In 1953 the first Technical College of Agriculture and Manufacturing Engineering was founded on the site, since the German Democratic Republic had adopted collective farming. The College educates manufacturing engineers to diploma status by direct, correspondence and evening studies. The house in which Hahnemann was born no longer exists, the space on which it stood now crossed by an extension of the original road, Neumarkt. On a house nearest the original site is a commemorative plaque and a bust of Samuel Hahnemann. At the end of Neumarkt, in the vicinity of St Nikolaikirche, there is a special Hahnemann monument, a granite pedestal on which stands a bronze bust designed by Professor E. P. Borner and erected in 1958. No Hahnemann museum exists, neither are there any special museums of homoeopathy.

Although the city has been largely rebuilt, Albrecht Castle, the Frauenkirche, the St Afrakirche, St Nikolaikirche, the Town Hall and the porcelain factory (now State-owned) still exist, and are now open to tourists, but the old City Theatre has been rebuilt as one of the most modern in the country. Meissen wine is still produced from the vines cultivated on the slopes of the hills, particularly the Spaar mountain. The original giant wine press is now in the city museum having been replaced by the modern installations of a wine co-operative.

A few days after his twentieth birthday, excited and somewhat apprehensive, Samuel bade a fond farewell to his family and took the mail coach to Leipzig, situated about 35 miles to the north-east of Meissen. There, he found himself accommodation and at Easter 1775 entered the University of Leipzig to study medicine.

The old University of Leipzig, founded in 1409, had by this time established a reputation as a centre of culture and learning, not only in Germany, but throughout the whole of civilized Europe. Many of its past scholars had become legendary; one such scholar, Goethe, had studied law at Leipzig only five years earlier, and it was here that he discovered his vocation as a poet and a philosopher.

In the same month that Samuel became a university student, the first shots were fired at Lexington to mark the beginning of the War of American Independence. George Washington was to issue the Declaration of Independence on 4 July 1776, whilst Samuel was still studying at Leipzig. On 12 June 1775, Captain Cook, who had joined the Royal Navy in the year that Samuel was born, arrived back in England in the *Endeavour*, having charted the coasts of New Zealand and the east coast of Australia. Like his contemporaries, Samuel did not realize the profound effect of these events in distant lands on world history.

Samuel had arrived at Leipzig clasping a large cloth bag, con-taining his spare clothes carefully folded by his mother, some paper, an assortment of quill pens and a purse containing 20 talers (about £8) given to him by his father. From this moment he became self-supporting and remained fiercely independent for the rest of his life. During his undergraduate days he maintained a meagre subsistence by teaching German and French, under-taking translations from Greek and English into German for comparatively rich students and, through an anonymous bene-factor in Meissen—probably Magister Müller—he obtained free passes to lectures. Thus, he achieved his independence. It is not certain that he ever visited his home again and he was rarely to visit his beloved Meissen.

During the winter months of 1775-76, Samuel worked in a single, sparsely furnished room, where he almost froze on bitter cold days. At times he would make himself a broth in which he soaked dry bread to soften it, and occasionally he would be invited to a students eating house (a kind of soup kitchen) when other boarders who normally used it were absent. Of some benefit to him at this time was his attention to his physical well-being, through regular outdoor physical exercise, 'to stand the strain of my mental exertion.'

The young undergraduate, Samuel, was soon to assert his individuality, attending his lectures on a selective basis. As he explained in his autobiography, 'only those I considered useful', which betrayed the independence of mind which was to characterize his later life. However, it is likely that this limited attendance at lectures was partly conditioned by his need to conserve his limited funds. Leipzig University did not meet his early expectations of stimulating, intellectual study. He was not able to indulge in the social life of the University as all his spare time in the evenings was spent in earning his own living; he translated at least four books from English into German during his stay. Neither did he form any lasting relationships with either his fellow students or his professors in the Faculty of Medicine. It is clear that he was disappointed in the lectures he received, and preferred more and more to acquire his knowledge from medical textbooks, thus increasing his isolation. He did, however, demonstrate his respect for one lecturer at least, a Professor Johann Zeune, in a light-hearted poem he wrote in Latin.

> Yet Zeune! on mighty wings shall fame,
> Be swiftly carried into all distant parts,
> He who through piety and mental vigour,
> The icebound spirit in us melts and moves.

His frustration was further increased by the absence of any practical facilities for his studies in medicine, as no hospital or clinic was available. It was this frustration in particular which decided him to leave Leipzig, late in 1776, for Vienna. In his autobiography he wrote, 'the inclination for the practical side of medicine, for which there was no institution in Leipzig, induced me to go to Vienna at my own expense.'

The old city of Vienna, capital of the Hapsburg empire, with its narrow streets still surrounded by fortifications, and the splendid thirteenth century cathedral of St Stephen, was at that time already recognized far and wide as a centre of the arts, music and learning. Mozart, a year younger than Samuel, gave several public recitals during his stay. Shortly after his arrival in Vienna, Samuel entered the hospital of The Brothers of Mercy in the suburb of Leopoldstadt, to work under the senior physician of the hospital, Dr Quarin, who was also a physician to the Empress Maria Theresa, ruler of the Hapsburg empire. Later he was to become physician to her son, Emperor Joseph II. In 1748 Dr Quarin founded the General Hospital in Vienna, which achieved world repute, and he was elected Rector of the University.

That Samuel, with his Protestant upbringing, should choose the Catholic Hospital with its patron, the intensely Catholic Empress Maria Theresa, speaks for Dr Quarin's reputation and Samuel's high regard for him. Later he related, 'I am indebted to the great practical genius of Dr Quarin. I had his friendship, I could almost say his love. I was the only one allowed to accompany him to his private patients'.

Thus, Samuel was to obtain the practical medical training which was denied him at Leipzig. In the light of subsequent events, however, he must have questioned, if only to himself at the time, the darker side of contemporary medical practice, with its blood-letting, leeches and nostrums, its lack of hygiene and its singular lack of compassion. His rebellion was in the embryo stage.

Towards the end of the summer of 1777, when Samuel had spent nine months under the tuition of Dr Quarin, from which he had benefited enormously, his financial situation had once more become acute, even though Dr Quarin had not charged him any fees. Samuel had been so engrossed in his work that he had not been able to earn in his spare time as he had done in Leipzig. As he himself put it, 'my last crumbs of subsistence were just about to vanish.'

He confided his problem with Dr Quarin who promised his help. Shortly afterwards the Governor of Transylvania (now part of Hungary), Baron Samuel von Brukenthal, recognized as one of the richest men in the country, came to Vienna on a political mission. Dr Quarin arranged for Samuel to be introduced to von Brukenthal, which led to the latter offering him a post as librarian and family physician at his home in Hermannstadt. In addition, Samuel would be required to classify his extensive coin collection. It was, perhaps, fortunate for Samuel that von Brukenthal was also a Saxon and a Protestant and his generous offer was therefore in keeping with his family motto, 'I will remain true to my nationality and my faith'. Samuel, not surprisingly, readily accepted the position and left Vienna for Hermannstadt a few days later.

The exact date of his arrival in Hermannstadt is not recorded, but the archives of the Masonic Lodge in that town reveal that Samuel Hahnemann (probably proposed by von Brukenthal, a Past Master of the Lodge) was admitted to the Lodge in the first degree on 16 October 1777. It is of interest to note that, although he did not pursue his masonic activities for many years after leaving Hermannstadt, he often signed himself in the masonic manner as Brother Hahnemann, demonstrating that he at least supported its precepts.

His stay in Hermannstadt lasted for one year and nine months. In the quiet seclusion of the library he gave his scholastic ability full rein. He catalogued the immense library of books and manuscripts, classified von Brukenthal's collection of coins, and practised medicine in the town. Apart from all this, he acquired an extensive knowledge of literature, furthered his scientific knowledge in botany and chemistry and studied several languages. He studied languages compulsively in that, when faced with a foreign manuscript or book of particular interest to him, he would set about a systematic study of that language. On leaving Hermannstadt he was competent in German, Latin, Greek, English and Spanish with a smattering of other languages.

It was, therefore, with some reluctance that Samuel left his honourable benefactor in order to complete his formal studies at the University of Erlangen, and he arrived in this provincial town (situated about ten miles north of Nuremburg in Bavaria) in the spring of 1779. He had just celebrated his twenty-fourth birthday.

His reasons for choosing the distant Erlangen rather than returning to Leipzig are a matter of conjecture. It is reasonable to suppose, however, that he was mindful of his frustrations whilst at Leipzig, in particular the lack of practical facilities and, although his financial situation on leaving Hermannstadt had improved considerably, the tuition fees at Erlangen were lower. Moreover, at this time, Erlangen would accept a late registration and required only a minimal period of residence at the University to qualify for admission to the final examinations.

Another reason for Hahnemann's choice of Erlangen has never been given consideration. The eighteenth century in Germany was a century of tremendous intellectual movement and turmoil. The rationalist school of scientists, scholars, philosophers, poets, dramatists and writers, including Goethe, Schiller, Wolff, Gellert, Lessing and Wieland stimulated the entire life of the nation in every facet, politically, spiritually, intellectually, socially and economically. The awakening of this critical spirit led to the movement called the *Aufklarung* (Illumination) and it brought into existence the free thinking, reformed Universities of Erlangen (1743), Halle (1694) and Göttingen (1737), where freedom of opinion and teaching were encouraged. These universities were formed to counter the narrow, orthodox approach of the older universities of Leipzig and Wittenburg. It is reasonable to suppose, therefore, that the scientist and scholar Hahnemann, the free thinking, intellectually frustrated deist, should be attracted to Erlangen. It is significant that he applied for a professorial post at another of these reformed universities, Göttingen, in his later life.

Samuel studied intensively throughout the Summer Term under a number of tutors, concentrating on botany under a Professor Schreber, to reach the required standard. He passed the final examination, termed the *Examen Rigorosum*, and submitted a relatively short, twenty-page thesis entitled 'Summary of the Conditions of Cramp According to Cause and Cure' with an appendix of a list of vegetable and mineral remedies, dated 1779. Following a verbal, viva voce examination before an Academic Board, he was awarded the degree of Doctor of Medicine on 10 August 1779.

At twenty-four years of age, Samuel Hahnemann was a pale, short but erect, young man of slight build with aquiline features, a narrow, curved nose and thinning fair hair. He possessed a brilliant mind and, as a philologist, he combined an exceptional scientific ability with a flair for languages. He was serious-minded and sensitive, pragmatic, fiercely independent and intensely religious, with an affinity for nature and his homeland. For his achievement thus far he was indebted first to his parents and later to his tutors, Müller and Quarin, and his benefactor, von Brukenthal, but not least to his own personal dedication and resolve to succeed against the odds.

3.

FIRST PRACTICES
(1779-1789)

A dedicated physician can only be sure about the healing
properties of a medicine when it is made as pure and perfect
as possible.

Dr Samuel Hahnemann set up his first practice in the small
mining town of Hettstedt in the summer of 1780. What he did in
the intervening year after he left the University of Erlangen is not
known; he never mentioned it in his autobiography and no
records have been traced. It is unlikely that he returned home to
be supported by his parents, for he remarked when he left for
Leipzig four years earlier that the money he had been given then
was 'the last money that I received from my father'. It is equally
unlikely that he engaged in postgraduate studies at Erlangen,
although it is possible that he gained practical medical experience, translated more books or gave language tuition in that
town. Bradford (1895), however, supported a theory, based on a
footnote by Hahnemann in his translation of Cullen's *Materia
Medica*, that he spent this time in lower Hungary. This obstinate
silence on Hahnemann's part in relation to this period of his life
demonstrated a distinct character trait. His obmutescence was to
reveal itself again over certain events and periods throughout his
life.

Why he chose Hettstedt, a small mining town on the River
Wipper, at the foot of the Harz Mountains and only a few miles
west of his father's and grandfather's birthplace, Lauchstadt, is
certain: 'the instinctive longing of a Saxon for his native soil. I
returned thither to begin my career as a practising physician in
the small mining town of Hettstedt in Mansfield', he commented
in his autobiography.

For five centuries the black copper-bearing slate had been hewn along the banks of the River Wipper, north to its junction with the River Saale, by the hammers and pickaxes of the miners of Hettstedt to earn them a meagre living. In all weathers, they sweated, strained and clawed for the ore, which yielded only a few pounds of copper per ton, inhaling its black dust which yellowed their skin. The squalor of their unhygienic and insanitary living conditions with its inevitable consequence of ill-health and suffering, depressed and frustrated the sensitive young doctor. In his first two-part essay (1781 and 1782), Hahnemann wrote of an outbreak of putrid catarrhal fever in the district:

> I am not daring too much when I maintain that, initially, epidemics are illnesses of isolated individuals, and that they are only *subjugated* by carelessness and ignorance. If I omit a prolonged spell of unhealthy weather conditions, penury and poverty, the remaining fault falls almost entirely on institutions, nurses and doctors, who alone by their bad behaviour change a medium illness into a serious one.

Copious withdrawal of blood by venesection, cupping or leeches was a regrettable feature of medical practice in the eighteenth and nineteenth centuries and, to a limited extent, even into the early part of the twentieth century. The thirst for blood-letting was nothing short of an insatiable mania. Blood was drawn in pounds. For the treatment of cholera, for example, 'it *must* be four or five pounds', recorded Dr Reiser. 'If insufficient blood is drawn', Bischoff instructed, 'the patient is still in danger of contracting a serious chronic disease, therefore it is necessary to repeat venesection, repeat it until the patient faints.' Generations of physicians considered it urgently necessary to venesect pregnant women in the firm conviction that it helped. In a notable case, an Italian nobleman died after five massive blood-lettings in two days, and when no more blood would flow, an artery was compressed to squeeze out another 'two or three ounces'. Even those suffering from complaints such as whooping cough did not escape the physician's knife—'for this condition, the earlier and more copiously the better', wrote Romberg in 1853.

It was said of the arch-protagonist of blood-letting, Dr Broussais (1722-1838), that he spilled more blood in his career than was spilled throughout the entire Napoleonic wars! Originally an Army surgeon, Broussais was the senior professor at the Military Hospital of Instruction in Paris, from 1820 onwards. His theory that blood-letting was indispensable to healing was carried to ridiculous lengths and, like many of his contemporaries, he believed that failure to carry out venesection should be a punishable offence. In spite' of Hahnemann's campaign against this practice, Broussais became a celebrated and popular physician. Later in his career, however, he acquired the nickname of the 'Medical Robespierre' on account of his mania. His most notorious case occurred in 1830, when the celebrated Goethe suffered 'a massive haemorrhage and he promptly drained another two pounds of blood from his patient.

In some hospitals the annual expenditure on blood-sucking leeches actually exceeded the amount spent on medicines! A dozen or more leeches would be applied to the affected parts of the victim—sometimes as many as sixty—and there they remained until their greedy, bloated bodies fell away. The breeding of leeches was a thriving trade in the nineteenth century. Official statistics show that in 1833 alone, France imported more than forty-one million leeches to supplement its own production. Those patients who survived the blood-letting or the leeches were inevitably left weak and debilitated and less able to combat their disease. Yet other forms of body purging were then applied to the victims—massive enemas, violent laxatives or nauseating emetics to induce vomiting. Then there were the medicines, many with serious side-effects, which were administered in massive doses.

These were the seeds of Hahnemann's discontent and subsequent rebellion. The inhumanity, the barbarism and the quackery of medical practice in his day appalled him. A typical day in Hahnemann's practice in Hettstedt was reconstructed by Humpert (1945):

> He was a bloodless old man with wrinkled yellow skin. The doctor took out his knife and opened a vein above the sufferer's elbow. He caught the spurts of blood in an earthenware vessel. He had only done what any doctor had been taught to do. The patient must have his vein opened to drain the disease from his body. A mighty shudder convulsed the sick man's body and they stood in the

ineffable silence, the poverty and arrogance of death. On returning to his surgery, the doctor covered sheets of paper with scruples, grains and drams of medicines: amber and cubella, Haller's Elixir, senna, aloes, oil of cajeput, bilge-water and the four liverworts. Then came the mustard baths and tartar emetics, the blood leeches swimming excitedly in water, for placing on the head and body and the cuppings on the neck, a vein opened in the foot and a clyster (enema) with vinegar, salt and mustard or asafoetida (resinous gum with a smell of garlic), a cantharidin plaster on the rump, a hot iron applied to the crotch, oatmeal possets, mistletoe powder for bleedings, red drops for convulsions.

'Here it was impossible to develop either mentally or physically', Hahnemann wrote and, in April 1781, after only nine months in Hettstedt, he departed for Dessau.

The larger town of Dessau, thirty miles from Hettstedt on the River Mielde near its junction with the Elbe, offered Hahnemann more scope for his intellectual leanings. He soon found a practice, and again satisfied his insatiable desire for learning by studying mining technology (his interest arising from his exposure to this industry at Hettstedt), and more importantly, by studying chemistry.

Chemistry, as a distinct science, had taken a great leap forward since Hahnemann's birth. The teachings of the Greek philosophers and the practical arts of the Egyptians and the Arabs gave way to the alchemists of medieval Europe, who were motivated by the desire to transmute base metals into gold and silver. Their search for the 'philosopher's stone' and the 'elixir of life' involved fraud and quackery on a grand scale. Van Helmont (1577-1644) and Boyle's work (1627-1691), however, represented the birth of modern theoretical chemistry, which replaced the unverified guesswork and mystique of the alchemists. They were the first to study chemistry for its own sake, and not as a means to make gold or medicines.

In Hahnemann's lifetime, Black (1755) and Cavendish (1766) were to identify the gases in air, and Priestley (1770) prepared several new gases. Priestley (1774), Lavoisier (1772) and Scheele (1770) made fundamental discoveries on combustion which overturned the 'phlogiston' theory and, in 1774, chlorine was discovered. Between 1781 and 1785, Priestley, Cavendish and Lavoisier established the composition of water, and subsequently it was decomposed into hydrogen and oxygen by electrolysis by Davy (1806). Henry's (1803) work on solubility of gases in liquids made a great contribution to physical chemistry and later he published his work on flame (1815). The quantitative laws of chemistry were propounded by Proust (1799), Dalton (1803) and Richter (1792). Dalton's atomic theory was enhanced by Avogadro (1811), and Berzelius (1811) confirmed the polar nature of elements in his electro-chemical theory, developed chemical nomenclature and determined critical atomic weights. Faraday published the laws of electrolysis in 1833.

It was not surprising, therefore, that Hahnemann turned his attention to the exciting developments in the field of chemistry and he was to become a skilful exponent in the years to come. Had he chosen chemistry rather than medicine for his career, un-doubtedly he would have made a significant contribution in this field. The famed chemist, Berzelius once remarked jocularly, 'That man [Hahnemann] would have made a great chemist, had he not turned out a great quack!'

In the second half of the eighteenth century there were two re-cognized public centres in every town where news, politics and business were discussed—the inn and the pharmacy. The pharmacist, or apothecary, and the vicar were the leading pillars of German society and these men would inevitably appear in every essay, book or play written in this period. The pharmacy was, traditionally, the morning rendezvous of the male popu-lation of the town, where news and gossip would be exchanged, business would be negotiated and people introduced to one another.

This social custom, which was particularly convenient for a young doctor wishing to establish a practice, together with his interest in chemistry, led Hahnemann to Haseler's pharmacy in Dessau. The apothecary of that name, who managed the business, was the stepfather of a girl of seventeen, named Johanna Henriette Leopoldine Küchler, with whom Hahnemann was soon to fall in love. Johanna was the daughter of the late Gotthard Heinrich Küchler (who had died in 1769), the apothecary who had formerly managed the pharmacy, and Marthe Sophien Küchler. Born in Dessau on 1 January 1764, Johanna was a charming, fresh faced girl with dark hair and large brown eyes, and it came as no surprise to their small circle of friends when her engagement to Samuel Hahnemann was announced. Humpert (1945), however, suggests that her parents were not particularly pleased and it is alleged they remarked, 'One doesn't marry an odd fellow like that!'

Samuel Hahnemann's impending marriage led him to accept a post, as he explained 'at a fairly substantial salary', as Medical Officer in Gommern, forty miles north along the Elbe, near Magdeburg. Having arranged for the banns of marriage to be read, he left his fiancée in Dessau and took up his new post late in 1781. Gommern was, like Hettstedt, only a small town consisting mainly of one long, densely populated street (Hahnemann came to detest having to walk this long street), with the remainder of its inhabitants widely scattered throughout a rural area. He found the work most congenial, however, leaving him considerable leisure time to continue his study of chemistry. So much spare time in fact, that he remarked that the town barely needed the services of a doctor. The reader will recall that his first medical essay was published during this period, in two parts in the journal *Medical Observations*, in which he described the outbreak of catarrhal fever in the district of Quenstadt.

After a year of bachelor existence and having rented a small house in Gommern, he returned to Dessau, and there at St John's Church, he married Johanna. The entry in the church register was as follows:

1782. On 17 November, Samuel Hahnemann, Doctor of Medicine, Medical Officer of Health to the Saxon Electorate in Gommern, aged twenty-eight years, eldest son [it will be recalled that his elder brother died in 1762] of Christian Gottfried Hahnemann, a painter in the porcelain factory of Meissen, and Johanne Christiana; with spinster Johanna Henriette Leopoldine Küchler, aged nineteen years [in fact she would not be nineteen until the following January], only legitimate daughter of Gotthard Heinrich Küchler who was apothecary here, and Marthe Sophien. The banns were published for the first time on 1 December 1781, and after the third time of asking the wedding was celebrated.

After the ceremony a small reception was held in the Haseler's flat above the pharmacy. It is not known whether Hahnemann's mother and father attended the wedding. We do not know that he had corresponded regularly with them, and with his favourite sister Charlotta since he left Meissen, and Rosa Hobhouse (1933) reported that he visited his home a month before his marriage. We also know, that his father's wedding present was an ivory fan handpainted by himself which Johanna was to retain all her life. Hahnemann wrote to a medical colleague shortly after the wedding, 'Both perfect each other, and love, mutual help, warning and advice help us to bear the burden of life easily and procure for us a condition as nearly akin to paradise as is possible on earth.'

So began the joys of home life for Hahnemann, with the love and companionship of Johanna, whom he later called affectionately 'Elise', which was to last for nearly forty-eight years. Johanna was also to share the hardship and the trials and tribulations of his turbulent career.

The days in Gommern passed happily enough. Certainly his rural practice did not provide him with sufficient income. Whereas the miners of Hettstedt could not afford his services, the country folk of Gommern were suspicious of strangers and doctors, particularly one so young as Dr Hahnemann, and they preferred to rely on their own traditional herbal remedies or even indulge in witchcraft. In those days in eighteenth century Germany, ignorance brought with it suspicion. Thus, every churchyard was believed to be haunted at night, every old house had its ghost and, although cruel executions of supposed witches had been discontinued, most old women living alone were believed to be associated with witchcraft and magic powers. Although he understood these people, to Hahnemann's rational, scientific mind these attitudes were totally unacceptable.

Hahnemann continued his study of chemistry in his leisure hours and translated into German a number of books on that subject, principally a work by the French chemist, Demarchy, entitled *The Wholesale Manufacture of Chemicals or the Science of Preparing Chemical Products in Factories*. The title of this book, published in 1784, augured the development of the chemical industry which was to change the face of Europe in the century which followed. Hahnemann's own annotations in this book were evidence of his increasing competence in chemistry.

In 1783 their first child was born, a daughter they named Henrietta (or Henriette) after her mother's second name. Like her mother, she grew to be strong willed, reserved and domesticated. Hahnemann's affection for his baby daughter is apparent from a lullaby he wrote for her.

> Sleep daughter, gently!
> The yellow bird chirps in the wood;
> Lightly it jumps over the ice and snow,
> And quietly sleeps in bare branches
> —so gently sleep.

Henrietta was destined to marry a minister of the church, Christian Peter Forster and live in Dresdorf, near Sangerhausen, where she bore two sons, Louis and Robert, and two daughters, Angeline and Adelheid. After being widowed she eventually died there.

Hahnemann's first original medical essay was published in Leipzig in 1784. This essay, entitled 'Directions for Curing Old Sores and Ulcers' (192 pages), demonstrated his growing disenchantment with his contemporary medical practice.

> It makes us more modest, that almost all our knowledge of the curative power of substances is mainly derived from the rude and automatic procedures of the common people, and that the wise physician draws conclusions from the effects of the so-called domestic remedies. . . . We treat cicatrizing old ulcers after many fruitless applications of salves, by causing several artificial sores; which only means exchanging one old wound for several.
>
> The majority of physicians refuse to treat this condition and leave it to the barber surgeon, to shepherds and hangmen, surely more from ignorance than disgust. The reputation of having accomplished such an heroic cure surpasses by far the smell of virulent pus. . . . In spite of this, my pride does not prevent me from confessing that veterinary surgeons are usually more successful, that is, have more skill in the treatment of old wounds than the most learned professors and members of the academies. . . . I wish I had their professional skill based on experience, which they have

frequently only acquired through treating animals. . . . So much is true and should make us more modest, that almost all our knowledge of the healing properties of the simple and natural, as well as artificial products, is derived from the crude and automatic applications of the ordinary man. . . . Their importance draws the conscientious physician more and more to simple nature amidst the rejoicing of his patients.

The essay also contained extensive references to the need for hygiene and recommendations for exercise and open air. Dudgeon (1854) mentioned that Hahnemann had even suggested in his essay that his patients would probably have done better without him. The young doctor was considerably encouraged by the reception his first important essay received. Professor Baldinger wrote in his review in his *Medical Journal* in 1785,

> The author has treated his subject very thoroughly and correctly. He shows how wrong the existing and most frequently employed treatment has been and teaches us a better way. The book is so thorough and practical that we cannot sufficiently desire that it may be much read.

In the same year, 1784, Hahnemann's father died. During the last two and a half years of his life, Gottfried Hahnemann had written a series of letters to the Elector of Saxony describing his experiments to remedy defects or cracks in the manufacture of porcelain and give it a firmer consistency. He also mentioned in the letters that he had been assisted by Samuel's younger brother August, who had become an apothecary. His last letter to the Elector, dated December 1784, begged him to allow him to retire owing to his failing eyesight. He did not live to enjoy his retirement. His last letter is filed in the archives of the porcelain factory, together with the statement: 'On 15 December the painter, Christian Gottfried Hahnemann, died in the sixty-sixth year of his age, after having been ill for only a week.' He was buried in Meissen on 18 or 19 December, 1784.

In his autobiography, Hahnemann wrote his father's obituary.

> He had found for himself the soundest conceptions of that which is good and can be called worthy of man. To act and to live without pretence or show was his most noteworthy precept. In his

actions he differentiated between noble and ignoble. His ideas on the first principles of creation, the dignity of mankind, and its lofty destiny, seemed consistent with his way of life.

His younger brother wrote from Königsbad, on 22 December 1784, 'The news of father's death will have touched you as it did me; we were both destined to mourn him from afar.' Hahnemann's mother wrote to her son, 'I am so weak from sickness and sorrow and worry that I am unable to go out and have to sit still in my chair.' However, her usual gregarious nature and contentment was again manifest in a letter to Samuel several months later, headed 'Meissen, 30 August 1785'. She described in great detail a visit, accompanied by his youngest sister Benjamina, to his elder sister Charlotta in Eisleben, reciting how she had ended a quarrel with her daughter and how long they had talked together.

But Hahnemann, his wife and young Henrietta had already left Gommern for Dresden. Their few personal possessions, carefully packed by Johanna, for the first of what was to be many times in the years ahead, accompanied them on the arduous hundred mile journey south-east along the course of the Elbe. On reaching Meissen, the coach would have paused in the market square in front of the Town Hall for a change of horses, probably not long enough, however, for Hahnemann to visit his family home, before setting out again on the road which hugged the west bank of the river for ten miles up the valley to Dresden. It may be assumed that the familiar sights of his boyhood—the distant hills, the old Frauenkirche, the castle, his schools, the *Rathaus*—filled him with nostalgia.

Why he moved to Dresden is not clear. Probably the rural environment of Gommern did not stimulate him intellectually nor offer opportunities for the advancement of his career. On the other hand, he had no post awaiting him in Dresden. By this time, however, he was already experiencing a growing frustration and a dawning recognition of a reactionary, obsolete medical profession, disfigured by ignorance. Whether he realized it or not, he was perhaps moving on to find an environment or situation where he could crystallize these thoughts and turn them into practical expression. 'Dresden', he said, 'was my next place of sojourn, where, however, I played no brilliant role, presumably because I did not wish to do so. Yet here I had no lack of friends or opportunities to learn.'

Johanna had, by this time recognized his strange, melancholic moods and apparent eccentricity and readily accepted his decision to move. They were to stay in the beautiful setting of the ancient city of Dresden, the capital of Saxony, with its many fine buildings—some still bearing the scars of the Prussian bombardment during the Seven Years War—its fountains and royal palaces, its libraries, museums, art galleries and magnificent cathedral, for more than four years, until the end of September, 1789.

Hahnemann's second child, a boy, Friedrich, was born in Dresden on 30 November 1786. Although he was well pleased with his first son and had great hopes for him, Friedrich was to prove a disappointment in his adult life, when he emigrated to England and later to Scotland, deserting his wife and daughter.

Friedrich was either born with a spinal deformity or became a hunchback as a result of a coach accident. Very talented, he wasted his potential, and in his later years it was reported (Knerr 1940) that he dressed rather freakishly in oriental clothes and became unkempt in his appearance. In his last letter to Dr Constantine Hering in America, shortly before he died, Hahnemann wrote, 'My poor Friedrich will become insane.' Friedrich died in Scotland, or possibly Missouri, U.S.A., aged eighty. His neglected daughter eventually married and returned to Dresden.

Apart from the pleasures of a growing family, Hahnemann found life in Dresden most congenial, with ample opportunity to further his studies which he tackled with renewed zeal. He continued to study science (retaining his special love for chemistry) and medicine largely through the medium of translating books on these subjects, which, almost incidentally as far as he was concerned, provided him with a source of income.

He made many friends, notably the Medical Officer of Health for Dresden, Dr Samuel Wagner, and the Superintendent of the Electoral Library, Hofrath Adelung. Dr Wagner, whom Hahnemann described as 'a model of unswerving uprightness', assisted him in his studies and introduced him to forensic medicine. The ageing physician was, however, overworked and ailing and, when he fell ill, he recommended to the Magistrates that Hahnemann should act as his locum tenens, to which they agreed.

The post of Medical Officer of Health carried varied duties including, *inter alia*, supervising the midwives and surgeons of the infirmary; treating the inmates of the military hospital, the workhouse, the orphanage and the prisons; submitting a medical report each month to the Mayor on all these institutions; investigating suicides and carrying out post-mortems; keeping down venereal diseases and rendering reports on criminals. The post also carried a paltry salary—Dr Wagner had more than once appealed to the Council for an increase but it had always been refused. However, since Hahnemann desired work and further medical experience more than improving his income, he readily accepted the challenge the temporary post presented.

Dr Wagner returned to his post after Hahnemann had carried out the duties for a full year, but he never properly regained his health and died in February 1788. Hahnemann promptly applied for the vacant post and the archives of the Health Department of the City Hall in Dresden reveal his application to the Magistrates.

> Greatly esteemed and noble Sirs, staunch, learned and most wise Guardians of the Law.
>
> It is an especial pleasure to me to offer you my services in the place of Dr Wagner. I should almost have hesitated to apply for so important an office which has become vacant, had it not been that your good will on the one side, and my great inclination for this branch of the profession on the other, had given me great courage. My literary work in connection with forensic medicine and the three years during which I held the post of Medical Officer at Gommern, are proofs of my suitability.
>
> I have the honour to remain, with deep esteem,
>
> > Your obedient servant,
> > Dr Samuel Hahnemann

The reason for his prompt application was the prevalence of putrid fever in the city, which necessitated the immediate replacement of Dr Wagner. It was Dresden's loss as well as Hahnemann's that his application was unsuccessful. The position was given to a Dr Johann Eckhardt, because he was older and more experienced

(Hahnemann had just celebrated his thirty-third birthday) and he had long been resident in Dresden. In any event, Dr Eckhardt died within a year of taking office, but Hahnemann did not re-apply for the position.

About the time Hahnemann's good friend and mentor, Dr Wagner, died, Johanna gave birth to their second daughter, Wilhelmina. Like her brother and sister, she was frail at birth. She died when only thirty years old, about 1818, after having a son named Hermann. Pleased as her parents were at her birth, it placed further strain on Hahnemann's meagre income. As it was, their diet consisted largely of sweet beer or milk, dry bread and groats, and Johanna had taken to knitting as many of their clothes as she could.

Each morning Hahnemann would leave their small, rented home in the Silzgasse and cross the bridge to seek the comparative peace and quiet, denied him by a young family at home, of the Electoral Library. Here he could further his studies, continue with his translations and write his books and articles on chemistry and medicine. Being a regular visitor to the library, he developed a friendship with the Library Superintendent, Hofrath Adelung (who was also a Councillor) and the Librarian, named Dassdorf. Hahnemann subsequently recorded in his auto-biography: 'Hofrath Adelung and Herr Dassdorf contributed a great deal to making my sojourn in Dresden interesting and agreeable.' It is noteworthy that in the eighteenth century German scholars developed a mania for libraries, and the post of Librarian was held in high esteem. Collections of 10,000 books or more became commonplace and, on his death in 1749, the Dresden theologian, Valentin Löscher, left no less than 50,000 books to the Electoral Library.

During his stay in Dresden, between 1785 and 1789, Hahnemann translated five major works: Demarchy's *Art of Distilling Liquor* and *The Art of the Manufacture of Liquor* (note that science was still considered to be a branch of the arts at this time); B. van den Sanden's *Signs of the Purity and Adulteration of Drugs* (Hahnemann was to have much to say on this subject in later years); Demarchy and Dubuisson's *The Manufacture of Liqueur*, from French, and, from the English; *The History of The Lives of Abelard and Heloise*. Why he departed from his medical and scientific sphere to translate the romantic life of these ill-fated lovers is not known, but it may have been at the instigation of Hofrath Adelung. The author must note here that, by a strange coincidence, Abelard and Heloise were reburied thirty years later in the same Paris cemetery as Hahnemann himself was to be reburied.

The truly prodigious work output of Hahnemann is demonstrated by the fact that these translations totalled no less than 1,780 pages. Furthermore, he so altered and added to the translation of van den Sanden's work that it became virtually his own. This particular work reveals Hahnemann's deep distrust of the integrity of many apothecaries (pharmacists) and the unreliability of their medicines. He also wrote nine articles on chemistry and medicine during this period, all published in a contemporary journal, *Crell's Chemical Annals* and a short book entitled *Prejudice Against Heating With Coal and Ways of Improving this Fuel*, published by Walther of Dresden. Suffice it to comment on these works only on their literary merit and the extent of his knowledge in fields extraneous to his profession. Then followed two full medical works: *On Poisoning by Arsenic—Its Treatment and Forensic Detection* and *Instructions for Surgeons on Venereal Diseases*, both published in Leipzig (1786 and 1789). The former attacked the standards of the medical profession.

> A number of causes for several centuries reduced the dignity of practical medicine to a wretched bread-winning, a glossing over of symptoms, a degrading commerce in prescriptions—God help us —to a trade that mixes the disciples of Hippocrates with the riffraff and medical rogues in such a way that one is indistinguishable from the other.

The reviews for these books were most encouraging. 'This book contains much that is good . . . the author has thought for himself and has written, not only thoroughly, but concisely and clearly', and another, 'This book is written with unusual technical knowledge, reflection and original thinking.'

A hint of his growing conviction that remedies should be prescribed in high dilution was given in his article. 'An Unusually Strong Remedy for Checking Putrefaction', published in 1788.

The particular remedy mentioned was silver nitrate for the treatment of chronic sores in a solution of one part in one thousand
with water.

Hahnemann made an indirect contribution to chemistry in
publishing a test for wine, which came to be officially adopted in
Prussia and known as 'Hahnemann's Wine Test'. The original
test, the Wurtemberg Wine Test, had been in use for nearly a
century for the detection of poisonous lead in wine arising from
adulteration by unscrupulous wine merchants in order to
sweeten it. The basis of the test was the precipitation of the
sulphides of lead, mercury, copper and tin by the addition of a
solution of hydrogen sulphide gas dissolved in water—a procedure widely used in modern qualitative inorganic chemical
analysis. Again he demonstrated his concern with adulteration
and impurities, which, in medicines, he believed would lower
their efficacy.

By this time, chemistry had become Hahnemann's prime
interest. He had now confirmed his earlier suspicions that the
medical profession as a whole was bigoted, corrupt and
reactionary and that medical practice was crude, barbaric
unhygienic, ineffective and lacking in compassion for suffering.
Although he was beginning to formulate certain theories to
remedy this situation, he was not yet ready to take positive
action. In any case, he had so far failed to find a permanent
position as a physician or any proper remuneration. It is not
surprising that he was becoming disenchanted with his chosen
profession.

On the other hand, unlike stagnant medical theory and
practice, Laviosier had overthrown the 'phlogiston' theory which
had stifled progress for over a century, and the science of
chemistry was taking a great leap forward. Inevitably,
Hahnemann found this stimulating atmosphere one which he
could not resist, and entered into it with gusto. Without doubt,
his literary works during this period made significant, original
contributions to chemical knowledge. Hahnemann's contribution to chemistry, however, proved to be only a prelude to his
epoch-making contribution to medicine.

His interest in chemistry was stimulated even more when he

met the celebrated French chemist, Antoine Lavoisier, on his visit to Dresden. The exact circumstances of the meeting are not known, but it is believed that it took place at a reception held at the Hotel de Pologne where he was staying. Lavoisier had made a great contribution to chemistry by demonstrating that on burning sulphur and phosphorus they increased in weight by the absorption of 'air', which he later showed to be oxygen. He later demonstrated, with Laplace, that water was a compound of hydrogen and oxygen. When he visited Dresden, he was at the peak of his career and held many important appointments in France, including that of Farmer General of Taxes and Director of the Government gunpowder factory. Soon after his return to Paris, however, the French Revolution began with the storming of the Bastille on 14 July 1789 and in July 1794, Lavoisier, along with the other Collectors of Taxes, was beheaded on the guillotine. Hahnemann was both distressed and depressed when he received the news in Molschleben, where he was then living.

There is some evidence to suggest that there was a short period when Hahnemann and his family, forced out of Dresden by high rents, lived in a farm cottage in the nearby village of Lockwitz. Finally, in September 1789, Hahnemann gave up his efforts to find a position or practice in Dresden and decided to move himself and his family to Leipzig. In his autobiography, he gave his reason for this move as 'in order to be nearer the source of science', revealing his intention to continue his studies still further.

4.

TRAVEL YEARS
(1789-1793)

The very smallest doses of medicines chosen for the
homoeopathic diseases are each a match for the corresponding
disorder. The physician will choose a homoeopathic remedy in
just so small a dose as will overcome the disease.

A few months after their arrival in Leipzig, the Hahnemann
family increased to six in number with the birth of their third
daughter, Amalie. Amalie, like all his daughters, was to receive
great affection from her father, but she became his favourite. Like
her mother, she too was to marry a doctor, Leopold Suss, whom,
unhappily, she was later to divorce. Her only son was also named
Leopold, and after the divorce he adopted the surname Suss-
Hahnemann in deference to his grandfather. He also studied
medicine and eventually set up a practice in London as Dr
Leopold Suss-Hahnemann. He retired to Ventnor in the Isle of
Wight, where he died in 1914, shortly after the outbreak of the
First World War.

Hahnemann's literary inclinations were well served by Leipzig.
He revived his associations with the University which he had
severed voluntarily some thirteen years before, when still an
undergraduate, and he became a regular user of the city library.
Not least important to Hahnemann were the famous Leipzig
printing houses; they were to publish most of his writings during
his stay. Indeed, Leipzig was to remain the centre of the German
printing trade until the Second World War.

In the absence of a practice and with little prospect of a medical
appointment in Leipzig, Hahnemann embarked upon a repetition of his esoterical life and work in Dresden: study, research,

translations and penning books and articles on chemistry and medicine.

He learned of the death of his mother in May 1790, in a letter from his elder sister, Charlotta. It came as no surprise to him since Charlotta, as the eldest child, had taken on the role of surrogate mother since the death of their father and, as such, she wrote to him regularly, keeping him informed of family matters and patching up disputes. Hahnemann's relationship with his mother had become strained in recent years. She had great affection for him, as he did for her, but with only a limited education herself, she failed to recognize the genius in her son or understand his enigmatic ways, which frustrated and annoyed her. Had not his father held a steady position all his life with a regular income? His father owned his own house—he had paid 437 talers for it! Moving from place to place—would he ever settle down? And those poor children!

Charlotta had written from Eisleben in 1788:

Dear Brother,
    Do not worry about the enclosed, which are sealed, they are mother's letters to August [his younger brother] and only contain complaints about you, that you do not love her, otherwise there is truly nothing in them. Act as if you knew nothing about it—she no longer writes like that, since you are now friendly towards her.

When his mother died, Charlotta wrote as follows:

1 June 1790.

Dear Brother,
    Thursday midday she left the visible world, she who bore us. Shed a tear in her memory, she was our mother. She loved you, dear brother, she gave you unmistakeable signs of it during the last years of her life. The tie which seemed to unite us, her three children, has been severed; on that account do not weaken the link of sisterly and brotherly love. You love me I know, be also kind to our sister, Benjamina. She will hand you the money left from the burial fund after the funeral expenses have been paid because our good mother wished you to have the money.

Her reference to *three* children (Charlotta, Samuel and Benjamina) suggests that their brother, August, may have died since the earlier letter quoted.

Whether he accepted the small legacy or not, Hahnemann's financial situation deteriorated even further. The arrival of their fourth daughter, Caroline, who was delicate like the rest of their children, was an added burden in their struggle against poverty. As it was suggested he had done in Dresden, Hahnemann moved out of the city into the rural environment of Stotteritz, a south-eastern suburb of Leipzig, where he could live more cheaply and give his children the benefit of fresh country air.

With no access to library facilities, he had no alternative but to work in the single room occupied by the whole family. To avoid the often noisy distractions of the children, most of his writing was done when they were asleep. Hahnemann's close friend in his latter years reported that he would work by candlelight in a corner of the ill-heated room, behind a curtain, until four or five o'clock in the morning. At least this left him free during the day to help Johanna with the chores, to play with the children and, between their lessons, to take Henrietta, who was now seven years old, and Friedrich, now five, for walks in the fresh air.

Based on accounts of relatives, Dudgeon (1854) reported on Hahnemann's life at Stotteritz, although he wrongly ascribed it to a later, more prosperous period in Machern:

> After toiling all day at his task of translating works for the press, he frequently assisted his brave-hearted wife to wash the family clothes at night and as they were unable to purchase soap they employed raw potatoes for this purpose. The quantity of bread he was able to earn by his writing for his large family was so small that he had to weigh out to each an equal portion. At this time, one of his daughters, a little girl (probably Henrietta) fell ill, and being unable to eat her portion of daily bread, she carefully put it away in a box, hoarding it up, child-like, until her appetite should return. Her sickness increasing, she felt sure she would not recover, so one day she told her favourite little sister (Wilhelmina, who was then aged four) that she knew she was going to die, and she would never be able to eat any more, and solemnly gave over to her as a gift the accumulated fragments of hard, dried-up bread.

Writing soon after their move to Stotteritz, Hahnemann reviewed his near desperate situation philosophically:

If I were single or had not five children it would be different, but in any case, elsewhere my expenses would be heavier. Besides, I am my own master here . . . what I now earn, little as it is, more than suffices me. I cannot reckon on much income from practice . . . I am too conscientious to prolong illness or make it appear more dangerous than it really is.

A year later he returned to this theme in another letter from Stotteritz:

It is impossible to live another year in this village. I cannot subsist on literature alone; moreover I have no suitable room for chemical work. I have to send for everything from the town by special messengers, except dry bread. I should have taken a house in Leipzig long ago, had not famine, unhealthy air and high rents driven me out of the town for the sake of my sickly children. Now that they are sturdy and strong, should I shut them up in the town atmosphere of Leipzig with all its expenses? Life there means almost unsurmountable hardships, especially with a crowd of five small children . . . now I know that my daily bread is assured by my writing, but I have nothing to spare . . . I have entirely given up my practice for the past year, because it cost me more than it brought in. . . . I want a place where I can live quietly and privately and yet can enlarge my knowledge as a scholar, surrounded by good people, and able to bring up my children straight and sensibly.

On a more spirited note, he wrote in his autobiography, written on the following day, 'Four daughters and one son together with my wife constitute the spice of life!'

It is noted with regret that Hahnemann's brief autobiography ended here, on 30 August 1791. However, from this time forward, his own medical and scientific writings and his followers would tell his story and, such was his ultimate fame, that his letters were treasured and retained for posterity by their recipients.

During this period in Leipzig and Stotteritz, from September 1789 until the summer of 1792, Hahnemann increased his activities as a writer still further. Urged on by the increasing needs of his family and, perhaps, by an innate sense of destiny, his output was even more prodigious than at Dresden. His two medical works and five chemical works were of particular significance. The first volume of The Friend of Health is worthy of special mention. In the introduction to this book he counselled public hygiene, which was to be a continuing theme. He protested against the prejudices, opinions and practices of his medical colleagues—another continuing theme in his future writings—and he protested against air pollution. In this connection, drawing upon his experience with his own family, he drew attention to the effects of town life in the upbringing of children. 'Fresh air, sensible diet, plenty of air, exercise and free movement are, as a general rule, always the preliminary conditions of well-being', he wrote.

These comments may seem obvious to us today, but measured against the living conditions and medical opinion of his day, Hahnemann was clearly ahead of his time. Haehl (1922) described Hahnemann's writing style: 'Even today it is a real pleasure to read these entertaining and instructive essays, in which Hahnemann shows himself to be a master of the German language. Grave, forcible and indignant when the need arises, yet full of humour and satire where the subject permits.'

His eight translations from English, French and Italian into German included a work of considerable significance, *A Treatise on Materia Medica* by Dr William Cullen. It was the second edition of this 1,170-page book, published in two volumes the year before in 1789, that Hahnemann translated. Dr Cullen was a leading teacher, chemist and physician in Edinburgh and was considered to be an authority on medicinal substances. It is probable, therefore, that it was on the initiative of the Leipzig publishers that Hahnemann was given the task of translating the work from English into German.

The special interest in this work lay not in Hahnemann's accurate translation but in his annotations, which showed he had succumbed to the temptation to experiment with one particular drug, cinchona bark (*Cortex peruvianus*), on himself. Cinchona or Peruvian bark had been used by the indigenous natives of South America for the treatment of malaria, and it had been brought to Europe by missionaries. It was given its name by the Swedish botanist, Linnaeus, from the Duchess of Cinchon, Vice Queen of Peru, who was cured by it. Dr Cullen stated—erroneously in Hahnemann's view—that its action depended on its tonic effect on the stomach.

For the first time Hahnemann recorded the effects of a medicine administered to a healthy person. This *proving* of the drug was critical and it foreshadowed his enunciation of one of the first principles of his new method of treatment—*homoeopathy*. A footnote by Hahnemann in the translation on the question of the efficacy of cinchona bark as a tonic for the stomach read:

> By combining the strongest bitters and the strongest astringents we can obtain a compound which, *in small doses*, possesses much more of both these properties than cinchona bark, and yet no fever specific can be made from such a compound. The undiscovered principle of the effect of cinchona bark is not easy to find. Let us consider substances which produce some kind of fever. I took, for several days, as an experiment, four drams of China [another name for cinchona], twice daily. My feet and fingertips, etc., at first became cold. I became languid and drowsy; then my heart began to palpitate; my pulse became quick and hard; an intolerable anxiety and trembling; prostration in all the limbs; pulsation in the head; redness of cheeks; thirst; briefly, these were all the symptoms usually associated with intermittent fever; all made their appearance. These symptoms lasted from two to three hours every time and recurred only when I repeated the dose. I discontinued the medicine and I was once more in good health.

In another note he recorded, '*Peruvian (cinchona) bark, which is used as a remedy for intermittent fever, acts because it can produce symptoms similar to those of intermittent fever in healthy people.*'

On a different tack, another annotation by Hahnemann in Cullen's works renewed his attack on the diabolical practice of blood-letting and purging: 'Blood-letting, fever remedies, tepid baths, lowering drinks, weakening diet, blood cleansing and everlasting aperients and clysters form the vicious circle in which the ordinary German physician turns.' Hahnemann's next attack on this practice appeared in the form of an article written by him in a newspaper called *Der Anzeiger*, published in Gotha on 31 March 1792. *Der Anzeiger* was often used by German physicians for articles and advertisements. In 1806 it became *Der Allegemeine Anzeiger der Deutsche*, and Hahnemann wrote several articles in the paper. This particular article, however, arose from the sudden death of Leopold II of Austria, the brother of Marie Antoinette.

He had succeeded his brother Joseph II (to whom his friend, Dr Quarin, was personal physician) only two years before.

Germany had been granting political asylum to many aristocratic refugees of the French Revolution, and the rest of Europe had looked to Emperor Leopold to exert his influence to avoid what seemed an imminent war between Germany and the angry revolutionaries in France. In view of the tense political situation it was deemed prudent to issue a special bulletin on his illness and death. Hahnemann wrote:

> Dr Lagusius [Leopold's physician] found a severe fever and a distended abdomen. He tried to fight the condition by venesection, and as this failed to give relief, he repeated the process three times more, without any better result. We ask, from a scientific point of view, according to what principles has anyone the right to order a second venesection when the first has failed to bring relief. As for the third, Heaven help us! But to draw blood for the fourth time when the three previous attempts failed. To abstract the fluid of life four times in twenty-four hours from a man who has lost flesh from mental over-work combined with continued diarrhoea without procuring relief for him. Science pales before this!

There followed considerable correspondence on this public attack on fellow members of his profession in *Der Anzeiger*, but although some supported Hahnemann—one even went so far as to write, 'Is not such a far-seeing, unprejudiced, cool and disinterested observer a representative of posterity?'—many were against him. Another physician who was also in attendance on Leopold promised to write a full answer to the charges, but he never kept his promise. To the Draconian doctors, Hahnemann's doctrine was an anathema. He was to take up the cudgels again on this subject with even greater zest in the years to come.

Evidence of a recognition of Hahnemann's qualities in some quarters at least were the honours conferred on him by his election to the membership of two learned societies—The Leipzig Economical Society and the Academy of Science of Mainz. Hahnemann wrote to the latter:

> To you I owe the unmerited distinction with which I have been honoured, through the Diploma of the Ducal Academy of Mainz.

Tender, please, to this exalted personage [the co-adjudicator] my best thanks and assure him of my obsequiousness, Samuel Hahnemann, 29 August 1791.

To Hahnemann this would seem a small consolation for his years of deprivation, but it was at least the start of a growing recognition.

It might have been Hahnemann's article in *Der Anzeiger*, which was published in Gotha, that brought him to the attention of Ernst, Duke of Saxe-Coburg-Gotha. On the other hand, it might have been Hahnemann's acquaintance with Councillor R. Z. Becker of Gotha, the editor of *Der Anzeiger*, for he too was a Freemason. Humpert (1945) suggested that they met in Leipzig when Becker visited one of his publishers.

Hahnemann had arrived with his family in Gotha, the capital of the Principality, about 150 miles south-west of Leipzig, in the spring of 1792. He had taken up temporary residence there while he was preparing to move on to Georgenthal to take up his new post.

Through constant division and sub-division the House of Saxe-Coburg had many branches. Since the eleventh century they had ruled over Meissen and Lower Saxony, and later Upper Saxony and Thuringia. In the fifteenth century the House was again divided between the brothers Albert and Ernst. Albert kept Meissen and the Saxon possessions under the title of Elector (later King), and Ernst ruled over Coburg and Thuringia. It was a descendant of the former branch that influenced Hahnemann's early life in Meissen and a descendant of the latter branch that brought him to Georgenthal in the Thuringer Wald. The announcement came in *Der Anzeiger* of 11 August 1792 by Councillor Becker.

To Friends of Sufferers
The nursing home for mental patients of the better classes, of which the preliminary announcement was made to the public in *Der Anzeiger* of 6 February 1792 has now been open for some time. A true father of his people (Duke Ernst of Saxe-Coburg-Gotha) found this proposition for the alleviation of human suffering so desirable that he gave up one of his country houses and had it furnished for that purpose . . . the locality where this home has come into existence is Georgenthal, an important village with a

law court and a forestry office. It is situated in one of the most
beautiful parts of the Principality of Gotha, at the foot of the
Thuringer Wald, three hours journey [nine miles] from the capital,
Gotha. The man who has taken charge of it is Dr Samuel
Hahnemann, to whom relatives and friends of those in need can
write for further information.

It was thus that Hahnemann became Manager of the Asylum
for the Insane. Even though his career had followed an erratic
course so far, this must surely have been the most unpredictable
step. Moreover, there are no records to suggest that the asylum
ever had more than one patient!

It is not certain when the asylum actually opened. The report in
February in *Der Anzeiger* mentioned that it had been open for
some time, although Hahnemann did not arrive in Gotha until
the spring and the patient, Herr Friedrich Klockenbring, was not
brought there until the end of June 1792. It is most likely that it
was opened specifically for Herr Klockenbring and the invitation
to the public to send their friends and relatives was an after-
thought. It seems that the initiative came from the wife of Herr
Klockenbring, the Minister of Police and Secretary to the
Chancellor of Hanover, who saw an article on a model asylum in
Councillor Becker's newspaper, and she was referred to Hahnemann by him. A respected official, Herr Klockenbring had shown
great eccentricity over five years and had been treated unsuccess-
fully by Dr Wichmann, the Hanover Court Physician, whom
Hahnemann described as 'one of the greatest physicians of our
age'.

It was the German dramatist Kotzebue who finally drove poor
Klockenbring into violent insanity. Kotzebue had written a
scurrilous and pornographic article entitled *Dr Bahrdt of the Iron
Forehead*, concerning an author named Karl Bahrdt, who in his
checkered career had been sent to prison, drunk heavily and was
the keeper of a brothel. The article named Herr Klockenbring as
one of Bahrdt's close associates and suggested that he had the
most dangerous venereal diseases and moral vices ranging from
drunkenness to fraud. The strain this article imposed upon Herr
Klockenbring, an official holding high office with a wife and
child, was too much for him. He became, therefore, the first and

only patient 'of the better classes' as the *Der Anzeiger* announcement put it, of the Asylum for the Insane at Georgenthal.

Hahnemann wrote of this episode three years later in the
Allgemeine Hom. Zeitung:

> After having been for several years much occupied with diseases of
> the most tedious and desperate character in general, and of all
> sorts of venereal disease, cachexies, hypochondriasis and insanity
> in particular, with the assistance of the excellent reigning Duke, I
> established a convalescent asylum for patients afflicted with such
> disorders, in Georgenthal, near Gotha.

Part of the experience to which he referred would have been
gained whilst acting as locum tenens for Dr Wagner in Dresden;
the duties of this post had included reporting on suicides and the
control of venereal diseases in the city. Dudgeon reported that
the 'great eccentricity' of Herr Klockenbring was due to overwork
and his 'fast life', and in view of Hahnemann's references to
venereal disease, it is probable that Kotzebue's allegations were
correct and Herr Klockenbring's symptoms were those of the
tertiary stage of syphilis. When he was brought to Georgenthal,
he was covered in large spots, imbecile and so violent that he was
escorted by two well-built men to keep him under control.

The conventional form of treatment of the insane in this period
involved more lunacy on the part of the doctors than that
exhibited by the patients themselves. The patients were treated
like wild animals; they were manacled and chained in dungeon-
like cells, abused, subjected to many forms of brutal corporal
punishment, including whipping, and treated with medicines,
the efficacy of which was judged by the degree of nausea and
vomiting they induced. A particularly crass and cruel 'treatment'
involved the strapping of maniacal patients onto a flat board
which was rotated or violently tilted between the horizontal and
vertical positions. It is noteworthy that these practices were slow
to fall into disrepute. A leading physician commented as late as
1880, 'What a short time has elapsed since the insane were shown
to the Sunday visitors of hospitals and workhouses as a sort of
sport, and prodded and teased in order to amuse the visitors.'
Another reformer named Reil wrote, 'We lock up these unhappy

beings like criminals in cells, in desolate caves or damp cellars. We leave them to decay in their own filth.'

Hahnemann's humanitarian principles caused him to reject these cruel treatments. His essay on his own compassionate approach summarized his attitude:

> I never allow any insane person to be punished by blows or other painful bodily chastisement, because there can be no punishment where there is no responsibility and because these patients deserve only pity and are made worse and not better by such rough treatment. The physician in charge of such unhappy people must have an attitude which inspires respect but also creates confidence. Their outbreaks of unreasonable anger should only arouse his sympathy for their pitiful state.

During the first two weeks, Hahnemann simply watched his patient, without treating him. He noticed the marks of the ropes that had previously been used to restrain him and left him free. In his ravings he tore off his clothes and broke most of the furniture, including a piano, but Hahnemann persisted in building up a rapport with his patient based on friendliness with firmness, and respect and confidence. He dissuaded Frau Klockenbring from visiting her husband as he thought that excitement or distraction would hinder recovery. Coupled with medication, of which he did not give any details, except a mention of tartar emetic, this form of psychiatric treatment eventually cured Klockenbring. It is recorded that on one occasion Hahnemann received a visit from Duke Ernst, accompanied by his elder son, Ernst, when they discussed Klockenbring's progress.

In February 1793, Hahnemann wrote to Frau Klockenbring with the good news that her husband was 'now quite normal' and invited her to come and fetch him. Friedrich Klockenbring left Georgenthal with his wife for Hanover in April, where in spite of his efforts to regain his former position, he was appointed to the lesser position of Director of the Hanover State Lottery. His health, however, began to deteriorate again and two years later, on 12 June 1795, he died at the age of fifty-three, no cause of death being recorded. Dudgeon, in his biography, claimed that Hahnemann had the honour of establishing the 'moral' treatment of the insane, but this was perhaps overstating the case.

During Hahnemann's stay, Johanna and his family had made their home in a wing of the hunting castle at Georgenthal. The spacious rooms and extensive gardens of this great country house were in marked contrast to the cramped conditions they had endured in one room at Stotteritz. Hahnemann's fees for his professional services included his living expenses and board for Klockenbring, which enabled Johanna to provide good, wholesome food for all of them, not least for Klockenbring himself, who had a gluttonous appetite during his treatment.

In a letter to Councillor Becker from Georgenthal, Hahnemann recorded that almost all their meals, including meat, vegetables, cereals and clothing, were brought daily from Gotha, as there was no store in Georgenthal. Johanna, with her usual domesticity, spent her days washing, cooking and caring for the needs of the children, whilst Hahnemann, between long tiring sessions with Klockenbring, would occasionally help Johanna with the washing or other household chores. He gave the three eldest children their lessons and sometimes he played with them in the gardens. A favourite game, which was very popular in eighteenth century Germany, was blindman's buff or *Blindekuhspiel*. He would also take them for nature walks to local beauty spots on the fringes of the Thuringer pine forests.

As he said before—'my family is the spice of life!' In all his travels thereafter he always sought houses with large gardens, and several letters from different homes referred to his beautiful or large garden. Hahnemann had by this time taken to smoking a pipe, whilst reading, which helped his concentration. By the spring of 1793, the children were sturdier than they had been in Leipzig and Stotteritz, and no longer sickly.

Hahnemann had written of his children's daily routine in his *Handbook for Mothers*. They rose at sunrise and were dressed in loose, comfortable clothes and allowed to get plenty of exercise in the fresh air, running about bareheaded and sometimes barefoot. They were encouraged not to be lazy and to train their senses and were helped to overcome their fear of darkness. He taught them to be polite, not to lie and to control their anger. They were not allowed to form bad habits and he insisted on regular eating and sleeping. The children were put to bed on hard beds at sunset.

Another chapter in the same book described Hahnemann's successful experience in teaching his children to read and write. First they looked at pictures, then practised the vowels and then the diphthongs and were taught to spell accurately. He taught them to draw all kinds of objects, including squares, triangles and circles, before allowing them to copy the less exciting letters and then to write words.

With the departure of Klockenbring and no new patients for the asylum, Hahnemann received 1,000 talers (about £400) in fees and was asked by the Duke's Council Chamber to leave the hunting castle. There was some criticism from Hahnemann's opponents for demanding what they considered to be too high a fee, but he maintained Klockenbring was a wealthy man, that he had a wife and five children to support and he had devoted his whole time to Klockenbring, without other patients and therefore no other income, with all the attendant risks of handling a sometimes violently insane person. He had no need, however, to demonstrate that his motives were not mercenary as he had often gone without food in Hettstedt, Gommern and elsewhere, rather than take payment from patients who could not afford it, or from those whom, in his opinion, he had not treated effectively.

The spring of 1793 was exceptionally cold and wintry, and Hahnemann had found no new position nor suitable alternative accommodation. In these circumstances he wrote to Duke Ernst on 17 April:

Your Ducal Eminence,

Will you deign me to put before you most humbly that the Council Chamber advised me a few days ago to leave the hunting castle now that I have given up the institution. I have made prepartions for this a long time ago, but I have been unable to find a suitable house, at a reasonable price, which would suffice for the accommodation of my rather numerous family. . . . I therefore take the liberty to beseech you most humbly to allow me to remain another month or two in your castle.

I remain in all submissiveness Your Eminence's most devoted servant,

Samuel Hahnemann

Duke Ernst, with his usual kindness, duly granted permission for Hahnemann to remain until 21 July. An amusing comment came from an intimate friend of the Duke, H. A. Reinhardt, who wrote in his autobiography that the local magistrate in Georgenthal was asked at this time how many lunatics Hahnemann had in his asylum. The witty magistrate replied, 'One, and that is himself!'.

At 8 a.m. on the last Monday in June 1793 (Haehl reported the time as mid-May) Hahnemann left their home in Georgenthal for Molschleben, a small village about fifteen miles to the north, travelling in a coach drawn by four horses, with Hahnemann and young Friedrich travelling on top and Johanna and the younger children inside. They were followed by a large cart drawn by three horses, which had been hired from the local innkeeper, and driven by the wife of one of Councillor Becker's servants. The cart carried all twenty-five hundredweight of their worldly possessions, loaded by Hahnemann and a labourer the previous evening. Hahnemann's good friend, Councillor Becker, had given him a bottle of good wine for the journey, which included a stop for provisions in Gotha.

After Hahnemann's departure from Georgenthal, the Dukes of Saxe-Coburg-Gotha were to experience mixed fortunes. The long French Revolutionary Wars and the Napoleonic Wars, from 1793 to 1815, were to bring them confusion, conflict and poverty. Ringed by warring countries—France, Prussia, Austria and Russia—the Principalities were in the line of advance or retreat of every army and the Dukes rarely backed the winning side. Napoleon himself once remarked in anger, 'Wherever I go I find a Saxe-Coburg in the ranks of the enemy!' On the other hand, the Dukes survived until 1918, largely through a number of well chosen marriages of their offspring into the Royal Houses of Europe. In 1817, the son of Hahnemann's benefactor, Duke Ernst of Saxe-Coburg-Gotha, married Princess Louise of Saxe-Gotha-Altenburg. Their eldest son Ernst was born in 1818; their second son, Albert, the following year. Prince Albert became Consort to Queen Victoria and the father of King Edward VII.

Hahnemann's own fortunes were also destined to be mixed, bringing conflict and poverty again, for his days at Georgenthal had been simply an interlude. He had begun his quixotic wander-ings, which were to be the feature of the next eighteen years of his life.

5.

WANDERING YEARS
(1793-1805)

But it is certain that the vital forces may achieve victory over diseases without inflicting losses on the body, provided they are assisted and directed in their action by a properly selected homoeopathic agent. It is nevertheless those vital forces that conquer in the same sense as a native army beats the enemy, although assisted by auxiliary troops.

Hahnemann was now thirty-eight years old and approaching middle age. He was not quite so erect as he had been, standing at about five feet eight inches tall, probably the result of many hours spent stooping over the candle to write and study. His thinning hair had given way to baldness, revealing his prominent forehead. His piercing eyes were still clear and shining, although now set deeper in a thinner face which accentuated his aquiline features.

Hahnemann's days at Georgenthal were only a brief respite. He had long since developed an antipathy towards medical practice as it then existed, with its rigid adherence to outdated methods. He abhorred the cruel practices and indifference to human suffering, the ignorance and incompetence and the hypocrisy. He believed in those things which today are accepted without question—the value of a proper diet, cleanliness and personal hygiene, of exercise and fresh air. He believed the hospitals were inadequate, poorly staffed, filthy and insanitary and his heart cried out for the plight of the unfortunate inmates of the workhouses, asylums and institutions. He despised the pharmacists, whom he considered to be corrupt, with their extortionate charges and the doubtful quality of their medicines. His idealism had caused him to refuse fees where he believed his treatment was inadequate or where his patients could not afford to pay, bringing privation to himself and his family. He was instinctively seeking a solution and to spread the knowledge to his fellow men. He believed that the answer to the cure of diseases and relief of suffering lay in nature itself, and that God had provided—but where and how?

> Though secrets hidden are all forbidden
> Till God means man to know
> We might be the men God meant should know . . .

Had a suitable post been available in Gotha, Hahnemann would have undoubtedly stayed after the closure of the asylum. He had often expressed his liking for this beautiful area and his respect for Duke Ernst. Indeed, several years later, in 1799, when he learned of the death of Dr Buchner, the physician to the Duke, he wrote to a confidant saying that he would like to return to Gotha, and of his intention to apply for the vacant position. As it was, he was now travelling to the small village of Molschleben to an uncertain future. It is likely that Molschleben was never intended to be more than a stopping place to a more distant destination, however. In a postscript to a letter to Councillor Becker shortly before leaving Georgenthal, he wrote, 'Do not forget the letter to your friend in Hamburg which is of such importance to me,' which suggested this city as his ultimate destination. Although his travels did eventually bring him to Hamburg, nevertheless, when he left Molschleben for Pyrmont in October 1794, he remarked in his first letter addressed from this town, 'Pyrmont, where I think I shall remain!' It may be significant that all his stopping places lay more or less in a straight line between Georgenthal and Hamburg.

Since travel and its implications were to dominate Hahnemann's life for many years to come, it is pertinent to consider the nature of travel in Germany at that time. In general, people did not travel more than absolutely necessary since it was primitive, difficult, costly and sometimes dangerous. A journey was regarded as an adventure which required much preparation and prayer, as it was a very lengthy and uncomfortable procedure, and there was a considerable risk of accident, robbery or violence.

When he was short of money, Hahnemann used the irregular services of the mail coaches, which were lumbering waggons, usually drawn by four horses or often shoved through deep ruts or quagmires at about four miles an hour. Generally, the mail coaches ran between the major towns about once a week or ten days. Passengers were usually besieged by friends and acquaintances to deliver objects, letters or parcels for them, which often resulted in the coach being dangerously overloaded and unstable. The journey would start from an appointed place, usually in front of the Town Hall, at irregular hours, as departure was dependent on sufficient passengers. Sometimes the coach would wait more than a day to fill vacant seats. The journey itself would be constantly interrupted by the need to water or change the horses, frequent repairs to the coach, collection of more passengers, becoming bogged down in mud, and often being held up by highwaymen in the remote country areas. In addition, the passengers were exposed for many lurching, bumping and bone-shaking hours to every extreme of weather. In more prosperous times and when his family grew larger, Hahnemann hired his own vehicles at special rates. He preferred not to cover more than about five miles a day and planned his own timetable.

Once settled in a very modern house in Molschleben, Hahnemann resumed his literary work, beginning with the preparation of the *Pharmaceutical Lexicon*, which eventually ran to four volumes. The lexicon proposed the ideal pharmacy of the future in which, *inter alia*, tinctures would be prepared from fresh, clean plant materials, poisons would be kept under lock and key and the preparation of the medicines carried out in a reliable manner, including safety precautions. It is remarkable that many of these basic precepts set down by Hahnemann are now incorporated in the provisions of the Medicines Act 1968, which governs the quality controls employed by licensed manufacturers of homoeo-pathic medicines today. The reviews for the *Pharmaceutical Lexicon* were most satisfactory.

> The author presents here a book which is very useful to the practical apothecary. . . . It compares favourably with similar writings . . . this work is not a mere compilation but contains many new ideas. (*Medizinisch Chirurgische Zeitung*).

A work of this kind by a man who had made a name for himself in chemistry deserves special mention. (ibid).

An excellent work which every apothecary ought to procure. Brevity, lucidity, decision and yet a completeness seem to distinguish this work. . . . This work will be of great service to the pharmacy. (*Journal of Pharmacy*).

Then followed an article published in *Intelligenzblatt de Allegemeine Lit. Zeitung* on the 'Wurtemburg and Hahnemann Wine Test', the 'Preparation of Cassel Yellow' and a 'New Wine Test'; these publications demonstrating Hahnemann's continued interest. in chemistry. An article written by Hahnemann in Molschleben, but not published until 1795, described his treatment of a number of children in the village for a disease known as milk scab. He isolated his own children, as he thought the disease was infectious, and successfully treated those afflicted by the application of a solution of *Hepar sulphuris* (powdered oyster shell fused with sulphur) to the sores. He mentioned that his own children, isolated as they were, and doubtless much stronger from their comparatively affluent period in Georgenthal, 'enjoyed perfect health'.

Johanna had been pregnant since leaving Georgenthal and, after a difficult confinement, she gave birth to their second son, Ernst, on 27 February 1794. The baby was baptized in the Hahnemann's home in Molschleben by Minister Gothardt, who later recorded that Hahnemann was the godparent, and the only one, to his own child, and he attended the baptism wearing a dressing gown and carpet slippers. That he should act as godparent is perhaps not so surprising as they could not have made many friends in Molschleben and their old friends were several days travel away. It may be assumed that the choice of the name Ernst was a mark of esteem to his erstwhile benefactor, the Duke Ernst of Saxe-Coburg-Gotha. Sadly, his parents joy was destined to be short-lived.

At this time Hahnemann was writing the first volume of *The Friend of Health*, which was published in Leipzig in 1795. Much of the material was drawn from his own experience when he was Medical Officer of Health in Dresden, and this had been supplemented by his subsequent experience, both in rich and poor areas. In those unscientific days people were always fatalistic and considered disease and epidemics unavoidable and virtually incurable. Ill health caused them to turn to all their superstitious beliefs and, not without some justification, there was an inherent mistrust of the physician's medicines. Smallpox, typhoid and tuberculosis killed tens of thousands of people, yet the value of a proper diet, personal hygiene, cleanliness in the home or a healthy environment never occurred to them. On the rearing of children, Hahnemann wrote:

> For the last twenty-five years we have watched these horrors and harmful degenerations. Baths in cold streams, in which the delicate offspring were plunged. They were forced to go barefoot and bareheaded, with uncovered chests over fields covered with frost, and allowed to sleep only for a few hours under light covers on hard beds.

On poverty, he wrote:

> This has brought many injurious habits to the world, one of the worst of which is where poor persons, especially women, sit over a vessel with redhot charcoal to avoid the expense of a stove. The closer the room is shut up, the more external air is excluded, the more fatal is this habit, for the air inside soon becomes a stupefying poison . . . when the person falls down the clothes are apt to catch on fire.

The desirability of fresh clean air and the need for public hygiene was a recurring theme in many of Hahnemann's writings both before and after this essay. He continued:

> If the Minister possesses no knowledge of sanitary police work; if the Mayor has no accurate idea of the rules regulating the prisons, workhouses and hospitals of his towns . . . if the bonds of married life are forged around the gay young girl before she has ever heard of the duties of a mother, then tell me whether there is any profession in the world to which does not belong a certain amount of medical knowledge for the respective care of the health of the individual or the family. . . . Fresh air, fresh water, free movement are, as a general rule, always the preliminary conditions of well-being.

Next to food, exercise is the most essential requirement of the animal mechanism—it is that alone which winds up the machinery. . . . Exercise and good air alone set up all the humours in our body in motion to fill their appointed places, and compel every secreting organ to give off its specific secretions, give power to the muscles and to the blood its deepest red colour; they refine its fluids so that they penetrate easily into the most minute capillary vessels, strengthen the heartbeats and bring about healthy digestion. They alone best invite us to rest and sleep, which is a time of refreshment for the production of new spirit and energy.

In the spring of 1794, after only ten months in Molschleben, the Hahnemann family were again on the move. This time the destination was the health resort of Pyrmont, nearly a hundred miles northward, the summer residence of princes and renowned for its mineral springs. In the early evening, when the coach was in the vicinity of the village of Mulhausen, disaster struck the family. With Hahnemann and Johanna and the six children packed inside the coach, the driver had whipped the four horses to gallop at excessive speed, causing the coach to lurch and sway violently behind them, until finally it swung outwards on a sharp bend where the road cut into a steep bank and overturned. With the wheels spinning above, the coach dragged to a halt in a cloud of dust, with the family in complete disarray and trapped inside. The children screamed in terror, but mercifully were only bruised and shaken. Dudgeon (1854) reported that the leg of one of his daughters was fractured. Hahnemann had a gash on the forehead, but the baby, Ernst, who had been in his mother's arms, received head injuries and went into a coma. Dudgeon also reported that many of their possessions were torn from the coach and damaged by falling into a stream below the road.

With the assistance of some peasants they made their way to Mulhausen, where they found an empty house for the night, and there they stayed for eight days, with Johanna in a state of severe shock and the children fearful of continuing the journey. Hahnemann wrote a few weeks later when they reached Göttingen:

I have stuck here in Göttingen and shall probably get no further. The upsetting of the carriage at Mulhausen in which we nearly lost our lives (to heal our wounds we had to remain there eight days) has shattered my wife's health so much and the children have become so afraid of driving, it is becoming impossible for me to come any further. The driver who overturned us is one of the most careless and dangerous men I have ever known. I hope no one else will suffer through him.

But the infant, Ernst, had already suffered through the driver's maniacal behaviour, for he died a few days later at less than three months old.

When they had recovered sufficiently, the family continued the journey to Göttingen, where they stayed for a short time. Not surprisingly, there was a hint of caution regarding his mode of travel in a letter Hahnemann wrote shortly before leaving for Pyrmont:

> I should be very glad if you could find out how much a good driver with four horses and a roomy carriage requires a day without my having to trouble about fodder. If I can agree with the man and like the carriage, and if the cost is cheap, I might use him. But I cannot decide on a definite length of road nor the number of days. On an average I drive not more than four or five miles a day and I decide my plans each day in order to be free to make just as short a journey as I like.

Dr Christian Pfaff became acquainted with Hahnemann at Göttingen, when he visited the local hospital. In his memoirs, Dr Pfaff wrote of his recollections and he described Hahnemann's arrival in Göttingen 'in a kind of emigrants carriage, together with his numerous family'. He also mentioned that Hahnemann gave him the impression of a 'mystic' and that he had treated one of his children for dysentery. From Pfaff's description, the treatment Hahnemann had already given his child was quite conventional, which indicated that, at that time, he had not formulated his new homoeopathic therapy.

The peripatetic Dr Hahnemann and his family were to stay in Pyrmont for only a few months, until early in 1795. Later the same year they were living in Brunswick and another daughter, Frederika, had been born with a still born twin sister. Frederika was to marry twice; first to a Court Post Secretary, Herr Andra, and second to a Clothing Inspector, Herr Dellbruck (although Bradford recorded in 1895 that they were one and the same man).

She died in 1835 in Stotteritz, where her father had lived previously.

About the time of Frederika's birth, Hahnemann learned in a letter from his sister Charlotta that his uncle, Christian August Hahnemann, the painter, had died in Meissen, aged 73 years.

Another move was foreshadowed when Hahnemann wrote a letter dated 21 June 1796: 'Sir, I notify herewith most submissively that I have sold my house and garden and pray you will withdraw the day for the auction sale. With fullest esteem. Your Obedient Servant, Dr Samuel Hahnemann.' He duly left Brunswick and stayed for a short time in Wolfenbuttel, a few miles to the south on the River Ocker, but in the same year he moved to Königslutter where remained until the summer of 1799. Königslutter lies ten miles east of Brunswick and only a few miles from Helmstedt, where the checkpoint now exists between West and East Germany, on the autobahn to Berlin.

Here Hahnemann wrote the second part of *The Friend of Health*, and he completed the *Pharmaceutical Lexicon*. He also wrote several essays, including the 'Pulverization of Ignatia Beans', 'New Principles for Ascertaining the Curative Powers of Drugs' and 'Antidotes to Some Heroic Vegetable Substances'. In the latter essay he explained that in earlier days physicians were looking for a universal antidote for poisons:

> At first there was enormous mixtures, then came the ineffective Bezoar and after that Gem Electuary. In more modern times, the universal antidote was sought in vinegar. Others saw milk and fatty substances as an alleged universal remedy; others relied on emetics. In the end they tried to find a corresponding antidote for each separate poison.

In addition, Hahnemann completed several translâtions, including Rousseau's *Handbook for Mothers*, from the French, and the *New Edinburgh Dispensatory*, from the English. Most of these writings were published in Leipzig. Again the reviewers of Hahnemann's writings were complimentary, and their comments suggested that he had by this time established a reputation for his work. For example, 'A work of this kind by a man who had made a name for himself in Germany as a chemist and as a practitioner, deserves special recommendation'. In Trommsdorff's *Journal of Pharmacy* a critic wrote of his translation of the *New Edinburgh Dispensatory*, 'The work is welcome, especially as the translation is an improvement on the English original on account of the notes by the learned Dr Hahnemann.'

Records of Hahnemann's life in Königslutter are almost non-existent. According to unconfirmed reports, his growing reputation as a doctor began to draw patients from far and wide, but many were attracted by the knowledge that he did not charge for the medicines which he produced himself, thus by-passing the apothecaries. The doctors in Königslutter, envious of his rising fame, mounted a vicious campaign against this itinerant interloper in their midst, and incited the apothecaries to bring an action against him for dispensing his own medicines. As a result Hahnemann was forbidden to prepare his own medicines and he was, once again, faced with the necessity to charge his patients for medicines produced by the corrupt apothecaries, in whom he had no faith. Paradoxically, his *Pharmaceutical Lexicon* was fast becoming a standard reference work with the apothecaries at this time! It is certain, however, that when he left Königslutter, he was depressed and miserable.

An insight into Hahnemann's erudition and his philosophy is given in a letter he wrote to a medical colleague:

> The ever beneficent Godhead animating the infinite universe dwells in us also, and gives us our faculty of reason as the highest, inestimable endowment, whilst from the fullness of His own moral character He implants in our conscience a spark of holiness. Even when we depart from this life, the great, unique, and infinite being, who suffuses happiness into all men, will continue to instruct us how to approach His perfect blessedness by further acts of goodness and to become more like Him to all eternity.

Of much greater significance, however, was his 'Essay on a New Principle for Ascertaining the Curative Power of Drugs and Some Examinations of Previous Principles', published in Hufeland's Journal in 1796 and subsequently translated in 'Lesser Writings'. Professor Christian Hufeland occupied the chair of medicine at the University of Jena, and Hahnemann was one of the first contributors to his newly founded *Journal of Practical Medicine*. Although Hufeland never entirely shared Hahnemann's views he was always ready to allow them to be aired and Hahnemann was to write many more essays for this journal in the years to come. In this particular essay, he outlined the three existing methods of healing.

> If I mistake not, practical medicine has devised three ways of applying remedies for the relief of disorders of the human body. The first method, that of removing or destroying the causes of the malady, that is preventive treatment. The second and most common, *contraria contraris*, that is, healing by opposites, such as the palliative treatment of constipation by laxatives.

He objected to the second method since he considered that, although it might offer relief at first, side-effects may occur if applied over a long period.

> I ask my colleagues to desert this way; it is the wrong one, a false pathway. The proud empiric takes it for the metalled roadway and puffs himself up with the miserable satisfaction of affording relief for some hours without any care as to whether the evil will take deeper root under this cover. And although the greater part of our medical contemporaries still adhere to this method, I do not fear to call it injurious and destructive.

The third method he described, used only by the more conscientious physicians of deeper insight, aims at achieving a cure by 'specific' means.

> One should proceed as rationally as possible by experiments of the medicines on the human body. Only by this means can the true nature, the real effect of the medicinal substance be discovered . . . every effective remedy incites in the human body an illness peculiar to itself . . . one should imitate nature, which, at times, heals a chronic disease by an additional one. One should apply in the disease to be healed, particularly if chronic, that remedy which is liable to stimulate another artificially produced disease as similar as possible; and the former will be healed—*similia similibus*—like with likes. That is, *in order to cure disease, we must seek medicines that can excite similar symptoms in the healthy human body*.

This enunciation of a new approach to medical treatment

attracted little attention at the time, but, although many would not agree, Haehl wrote in 1922, 'the fact remains that 1796 is the year of the birth of homoeopathy'. In the same year, Dr Edward Jenner, who practised in Gloucestershire, had inoculated a young boy with cow pox against small pox and thus demonstrated the principle of immunization. *Similia similibus?* This idea had already been considered by Hahnemann, but he had rejected it because of the risks involved in introducing matter derived from disease. The word 'homoeopathy' was devised by Hahnemann some years later from the Greek word *homoios*—similar, and *pathos*—disease; thus 'similar disease', or the treatment of like with like. The word 'homoeopathic' appeared for the first time in his essay 'Indications of the Homoeopathic Employment of Medicines in Ordinary Practice', published in Hufeland's Journal in 1807.

The paucity of information over these years of Hahnemann's life was the result of one of his now characteristic obstinate silences; only a hint of his activities may be gleaned from his occasional letters. With his nomadic existence, even the source of some of these letters is in doubt, but his silence is quite understandable, as it was not a particularly happy period for him or his family, and certainly some experiences, such as the death of Ernst, he would have wished to forget.

Hahnemann's journeys northward during the years 1793 to 1799 took him across the axis of advance and retreat of warring armies, and he and his family must have been exposed to considerable danger, particularly when travelling on the open road. The dangers would have been familiar to Hahnemann, for he had experienced this situation in his youth during the Seven Years War. They would have been subject to curfew, and prey to straggling bands of soldiers of the different armies intent on looting or rape, in addition to highwaymen who exploited the confusion which arose, and the constant breakdowns in law and order.

In 1792, the tumult of the French Revolution had reached its height, with the mobs in the streets of Paris, which rang with the strains of the *Marseillaise*. Prussia had declared war on France in support of Austria; its troops had advanced and captured

Longwy and then Verdun, only to suffer defeat by the French Army at Valmy. The end of the monarchy was proclaimed and the head of Louis XVI fell under the guillotine in January 1793. French armies then embarked on widespread republican aggression in Holland and the German principalities, including Coburg, Gotha and Hahnemann's beloved Saxony.

Old conventions were flung to the winds. Following the Reign of Terror, and with Paris near to anarchy, in October 1795 the Directory had appointed a young artillery officer, Napoleon Bonaparte, to disperse the mobs and establish their authority. The future dictator was rewarded with the command of the French armies in Italy and proceeded to 'liberate' the north of that country. But Napoleon had underrated the effectiveness of sea power manifested by Britain and, having embarked on his Egyptian expedition in 1798, the French fleet was tracked down and annihilated by Horatio Nelson in the Battle of the Nile. Undeterred, Napoleon carried out his *coup d'état* of Brumaire in November 1799, and thus established his absolute dictatorship.

Hahnemann's attitude was summed up when, after leaving Hamburg, he wrote, 'Oh! if we had only escaped the war, which is the graveyard of science!' Years later, when the Napoleonic Wars were coming to an end, he wrote to his friend Dr Stapf, 'If this wicked war would only leave us in peace so that we might print something! Then we might take a new lease of life.' In a rare political comment, Hahnemann wrote:

> I am of the opinion that times will soon be better. In our previous state of subjugation, everybody was silent, especially the good people. The better minds had been so intimidated and disheartened that they dare not express their feelings. Only the voice of the common mob was heard, glad in the general depravity to be able to suppress the best in speech and writing as exemplified by the suppressor of all—Napoleon!

On his arrival in Königslutter, in October 1797, Hahnemann had placed an advertisement in *Der Anzeiger* in an attempt to find a position which would enable him to return to Gotha. In March 1799, he wrote again to his old friend, Councillor Becker in Gotha, in a vain attempt to secure the position of physician to Duke Ernst of Saxe-Coburg-Gotha.

Yet another move was inevitable. After a brief stay in Hamburg, the 'emigrants carriage, together with his numerous family', as Dr Pfaff had described, duly arrived, at the rented house in the suburbs of Altona, near Hamburg, which was to be their home for only a few weeks. The contact in Hamburg, to whom Councillor Becker had written when Hahnemann left Gotha, failed to find him a suitable position.

Whilst practising in Altona, Hahnemann was inundated with requests from people taking advantage of his good nature, seeking free advice. With his income no longer subsidized by the fee he had received for his services to Herr Klockenbring in Georgenthal, he was again faced with financial problems. In view of these problems, he became so annoyed with these demands for gratuitous advice that he wrote the following letter, which he paid to have inserted, in *Der Reichanzeiger*:

Dear Public!

It will scarcely be credited that there are people who seem to think that I am merely a private gentleman with plenty of time on my hands, whom they may pester with letters, many of which have not the postage paid, and are consequently a tax on my purse, containing requests for professional advice, to comply with which would demand much mental labour and occupy precious time, while it never occurs to these inconsiderate correspondents to send any remuneration for the time and trouble I would have to expend on answers by which they would benefit.

In consequence of the ever-increasing importunity of these persons, I am compelled to announce:

1. That henceforward I shall refuse to take in any letters which are not postpaid, let them come from whom they may.
2. That after reading through even paid letters from distant patients and others seeking advice, I will send them back unless they are accompanied by a sufficient fee (at least one gold piece) in a cheque or actual money, unless the poverty of the writer is so great that I could not hold back my advice without sinning against humanity.
3. If lottery tickets are sent to me I shall return them all without exception: but I shall make the post office pay for all the expenses of remission and the senders will get them back charged with this payment.

Altona, by Hamburg   Samuel Hahnemann,
9 November 1799   Doctor of Medicine

This letter aroused considerable criticism, since it was contrary to accepted practice at that time, and it gave his medical contemporaries a further opportunity for cavilling against him. Several highly critical—and hypocritical—letters were published in *Der Reichanzeiger*, shortly afterwards.

Another unfortunate episode added to Hahnemann's problems at this time when, at the suggestion of Councillor Becker, he received a mental patient into his home in Altona. For nine gold pieces a month he treated a certain Johann Karl Wezel, an Austrian dramatist, but his wild behaviour, which upset Johanna and the children, coupled with his enormous appetite, forced Hahnemann to beg his old friend to take the patient away after only eight weeks.

Hahnemann's next move, to St Jurgen, just outside Hamburg, was presaged in one of his regular letters to Councillor Becker in Gotha:

Altona, 16 April 1800

Dearest Friend,
    At last! you will think, and you are right. The times for my moving are Ascension Day and on St Martins Day. I shall, therefore, only get out of this house, which I am renting, in five weeks time. It is now sold, and in any case is no longer suitable for me. That I am not staying in Altona or Hamburg you have already seen from my previous letter. Non-payment of debts, swindling and famine have reached their highest record. I should grow tired of my life if I remain here.

Robert Browning could have had Hahnemann in mind when he penned:

One who never turned his back but marched breast forward,
Never doubted clouds would break,
Never dreamed, though right were worsted, wrong would
    triumph.

Hahnemann's first letter from their next stopping place, Mölln, a village of only 230 houses nine miles south of the port of Lubeck, was dated 21 September 1800. 'Expensive Hamburg nearly swallowed me up', Hahnemann commented, no doubt conscious of the inflation, corruption and a black market in goods that war had brought in its wake. In Mölln, Hahnemann decided to devote himself once more solely to his writing and not to 'practise by the way', as he put it. It is worth noting that this was the most northerly point Hahnemann was to reach in his life, for from this time on, his travels took him south, not surprisingly, back to Saxony.

Here Hahnemann and his family would have had their first, and for Johanna and himself their only, glimpse of the sea. They remained in Mölln for only a few weeks, moving to Machern, four hours coach journey north-west from Leipzig, in the winter of 1800-1801.

Another brief stay in nearby Eilenburg, then to Wittenburg on the River Elbe, and finally to Johanna's home town of Dessau for the first time since they were married there, some twenty years before. The dates of these restless wanderings are extremely vague, and only an occasional letter gave any hint of their dwelling place or mode of living.

At this juncture it might be appropriate to consider the contribution of Hahnemann's loving and loyal wife, Johanna, on whom he relied for his physical, mental and spiritual support during his long travels. She was now rather plump and her round, motherly face was etched with lines from the worry, toil and privation she had experienced over the years. She had borne eight children, one stillborn and another killed, and raised the others through their formative years, coping with their problems prudently and unselfishly. Henrietta was now 21, Friedrich 18, Wilhelmina 16, Amalie 15, Caroline 13 and Frederika 9 years old. She was yet to bear three more children!

Johanna had moved with her family and their possessions at least twenty times in those twenty years — Dessau — Gommern — Leipzig — Dresden — Leipzig — Stotteritz — Georgenthal — Molschleben — Mulhausen — Pyrmont — Wolfenbüttel — Brunswick — Königslutter — Hamburg — Altona — St Jurgen — Mölln — Machern — Eilenburg — Wittenburg — Dessau. Even by today's standards this would have been a staggering feat, but measured against the standards of the late eighteenth century, with its wartime dangers, poverty and famine, primitive sanitary arrangements, inadequate heating and arduous travel, her

4. Map showing Hahnemann's many places of residence.

5. Johanna Henriette Leopoldine Hahnemann.

achievement was indeed remarkable. Yet, throughout all this time, she had coped with the perverse moods of her husband, the frustrated, unsettled, idiosyncratic genius, Samuel Hahnemann, with understanding, affection, help and encouragement.

Albrecht wrote of Johanna:

> Hahnemann had his daughters carefully trained and educated. They were also well·instructed by their mother in all the domestic and womanly occupations, as also in household management. Johanna had generally a greater influence than the father during the time they remained in their parents house. She was a capable woman, of energetic character, of unusually high culture for those days, and of a great personal kindness. . . . She lived solely for her family.

In 1865, Reichardt wrote of her:

> Johanna Henriette Leopoldine sacrificed to him her whole property. . . . She was the thoughtful housewife, the faithful mother, who must have been full of anxiety when she considered what would become of her large family if Hahnemann could not resolve his problems satisfactorily. Johanna Henriette Leopoldine watched with tender care over the domestic happiness and tranquil peace of her husband, so that he only felt happy in his home, in his family and seldom left them!

Gordon Ross (1976) made a harsh judgement on Johanna when he suggested that the tragic death of Ernst, the emigration of Friedrich and the divorce of three of her daughters 'showed that she did not make a very good job of bringing up her large brood.' He also commented that Hahnemann's daughters had the hard German nature of their mother. Even Haehl (1922) wrote, 'A strong reign of harshness was due to end with the passing of *this woman*, whose whole life was retirement, work and economy. She was a good German housewife, and did not wish to be anything more.' To be quite fair, however, it must be remembered that in those days, women were not given the opportunity, nor did society tolerate them being anything else.

It was variously reported, however, that, particularly in her later years, Johanna became very domineering and nagged her husband incessantly for not doing like other doctors and earning a good, regular income to support his family properly. Whether this was true or not, no small share of the credit for Hahnemann's ultimate contribution to medicine must be attributed to her.

Hartmann, in his biography of 1844, wrote in typical Victorian phraseology: 'Notwithstanding the multiplicity of inquiry and research, it cannot be ascertained how long Hahnemann resided at Eilenburg, nor is it even known how long he lived at Machern.' We know, however, from definite sources that the following works were written during his stay of about two years at Dessau (Haehl, in 1922, disagreed and insisted the period was only a few months), where he had gone from Wittenburg: *Coffee and its Effects* (published in Leipzig, 1803), *Aesculapius in the Balance* (Leipzig, 1805), *Medicine of Experience* (Berlin 1805), a forerunner of his *Organon*, and *Fragmenta de Viribus Medicamentorum* (Leipzig 1805). To these writing we can now add: *Some Kinds of Continued and Remittent Fevers* (1797), *Cure and Preventing of Scarlet Fever* (published in Gotha by Becker 1801), 'On the Power of Small Doses of Medicine in General and of Belladonna in Particular' (Hufeland's Journal 1801), 'Fragmentary Observations on Brown's Elements of Medicine' (Hufeland's Journal, 1810) and an essay on 'A New Alkaline Salt, Alkali Pneum' (published in *Allegemeine Literaturzeitung* and two other journals 1801).

These writings were of fundamental importance in that they included many statements which demonstrated that his new system of medical therapy was being formulated in his mind, although not yet brought together into a coherent system. They did, however, result in a mistake and lead to further conflict with the medical profession. The mistake occurred with his announcement in his essay, 'A New Alkaline Salt, Alkali Pneum', that he had discovered a new chemical compound which could be of medicinal value and that it could be obtained from an address in Leipzig for a certain sum of money.

The Society of Friends of Natural Science of Berlin became interested in this new discovery and purchased a one-ounce sample. The phial, labelled 'Alkali Pneum' and carrying Hahnemann's seal, was opened and the contents tested, but the report showed that it was a neutral salt with a preponderance of sodium. In fact, it was common borax. The report said: 'We hope Dr Hahnemann will publish for his own justification how he was misled into announcing such a well-known and common substance as borax under the heading of a new discovery and to offer it for sale at such a price, when it could be obtained at any chemists shop for a few pence.'

The apothecaries, still smarting from Hahnemann's previous attacks on their integrity and competence, were swift to take their revenge, and insulting remarks and derisory articles soon appeared in a number of journals. An article by an apothecary in *Crells Annals* criticized Hahnemann's 'great mistake' and Dr Trommsdorf, a Professor of Chemistry and an apothecary, wrote in *Der Reichsanzeiger*, in an article entitled 'Unexpected Shamelessness of Dr Samuel Hahnemann':

> That this salt was nothing but borax, Hahnemann ought to have known, or be accused of the most glaring chemical ignorance. . . . A great deal of impudence is required to pull the leg of the worthy German chemical fraternity, and to defraud them of their money. . . . What will foreigners say, and what are the prospects of the future trustworthiness of Dr Hahnemann?

Hahnemann wrote in his defence in *Scherer's Journal of Chemistry*, 'I am incapable of wilfully deceiving; I may, however, be unintentionally mistaken. I am in the same boat as others before me' (several famous chemists, such as Proust, had erroneously claimed to have found new compounds). Hahnemann then gave a detailed account of his experimental procedure to isolate the compound, and the cause of the error. He then gave the money he had received for the sample to a charity in Leipzig. He had readily admitted his mistake and had done his best to rectify it. Some years later he wrote, 'If I had once made a chemical error—for to err is human—I was at any rate the first to retract it.' Hahnemann had at least one supporter in a Professor August Scherer, who defended him in *Der Reichsanzeiger*, 'Why did not Professor Trommsdorf of Erfurt first wait for his defence before making such an exceedingly ill-natured and intolerant attack on Hahnemann? Everyone who, like myself knows him, will acknowledge that Dr Hahnemann is an upright and truth-loving man. Has Professor Trommsdorf never made a mistake?'

It was unfortunate that Hahnemann had laid himself open to this attack since he was already being pilloried by the obscurant doctors on account of his publication *Cure and Prevention of Scarlet Fever* (1801). As a result, the apothecaries were quick to align themselves with the doctors against their old adversary. In this pamphlet, Hahnemann wrote of the nature of scarlet fever and his experiences in treating the disease during an outbreak which occurred when he was living in Königslutter. He gave details of the preparation of his antidote, *Belladonna*. Three children in a family had contracted scarlet fever. Hahnemann noticed that a fourth child, who had been taking *Belladonna* for another complaint, did not catch the disease. Therefore, he gave *Belladonna* in very small doses (one four hundred and thirty-two thousandth part of a grain) to the remaining members of this family, as a prophylactic, and repeated the dose every three days. None of the family treated in this way contracted the disease and Hahnemann concluded that a remedy which can rapidly cure at the onset of an illness must be the best preventive.

But Hahnemann's new form of treatment proved to be a Pyrrhic success. It was even more unfortunate that he had pre-empted this publication by a letter, published in *Der Reichanzeiger* in April 1800, in which he stated that he was about to issue a pamphlet giving a complete history of the scarlet fever epidemic in Königslutter. But he also stated that he would only give the name of the remedy he used, and the method of preparation and the treatment if he received the sum of one gold piece from three hundred subscribers. To each subscriber he promised he would supply a quantity of the remedy and directions for its use. The letter produced only forty subscribers, and in the following month, Hahnemann had a further letter published in *Der Reichanzeiger*:

> The demand to introduce my remedy for scarlet fever infection, as soon as possible, becomes more insistent. It is making an appeal to my conscience, seeing that scarlet fever is raging. . . . But no one who is reasonable can expect me to neglect my own interests in order to fulfil this legitimate request on the part of the public, by urging that it is my duty to acquiesce in their desire without having due regard to my own claims. It is certainly worth something to

have found forty subscribers, but that is still far below the three hundred whom I may reasonably expect. . . . Meanwhile, there is, however, an alternative for those who are now suffering which will prove my sympathy for the welfare of humanity. I have deposited in the office of *Der Reichanzeiger*, my remedy, made up in small powders. Everyone who deposits a gold piece, as a subscription to my book on scarlet fever, will receive such a little powder free of charge, which contains enough to render several thousand people immune from scarlet fever, with the receipt for his money.

With the letter for publication Hahnemann enclosed a personal letter to his old friend, Councillor Becker.

Altona, 1 May 1800

Dearest Friend,

I believe that I have now found out how to steer a middle course by means of the enclosed announcement, which I beg you to insert as soon as possible, for the sake of those who are suffering, so that the world may be served, and that I at the same time not be forgotten. . . . If previous subscribers should ask for the powders, please do not refuse them. Put expense and trouble to my account . . . no one can expect me to forget myself, especially with a numerous family and considering the many sacrifices I have already made gratuitously. On Ascension Day I shall be settled down in a pretty house in St Jurgen, near Hamburg . . . I shall move in two weeks time. Kind regards and best wishes for your health. Kind greetings from my family to you all.

Dr Hahnemann

Predictably, abusive and indignant letters poured into the offices of *Der Reichanzeiger*. Hahnemann was criticized for demanding payment in advance, for keeping the remedy secret, that the substance he used was highly toxic and that such a small dose could not possibly be efficacious. In the face of this storm of protest, even his friend, Councillor Becker, wavered in his support, which prompted Hahnemann to write to him in an undated letter:

Just confess frankly that your attitude towards me has changed, but I beg you as a last favour to explain to me the causes of this change. I long at least for your frank declaration that you feel coldly towards me, and that the only support which seems to be left to me in this country has been shattered.

This episode presents a striking example of Hahnemann's enigmatic disposition. It might suggest a conflict between his experience and intellect, between his idealism and reality, or plain economic necessity. His overt mercenary attitude in this matter was in sharp contrast to his compassion for suffering and his refusal to charge his poorer patients, or his refusal to charge when he considered his treatment was inadequate. He was, no doubt, conditioned by the persistent persecution of the doctors and the apothecaries and, in any case, in his opinion they would certainly have charged extortionate fees had they been in possession of his cure. Certainly his rebellion was born from his professional discontent. What frustrated him was that his professional colleagues could not, or did not try to, *understand* him.

The Hahnemanns' ninth child and sixth daughter, Eleonore, was born in 1803 during their stay in Dessau. She eventually married a certain Herr Klemmen and after his death she married a Dr Wolff. She divorced her second husband, and died in tragic circumstances in Köthen, where she had lived for many years after her father had left the town.

From early in 1805, letters written by Hahnemann, giving his address in the Pfarrgasse in Torgau, confirmed that he had moved once again. The strategically situated, walled town of Torgau spans the River Elbe and lies about midway between Dessau to the north-west and Meissen to the south-east. Here he had set up his practice in a freehold house with a drive and garden, which he had bought.

Happily for Johanna, who was now expecting another child, and the children, Hahnemann was about to enter a more settled period in his life. He remained in Torgau for nearly seven years. His proclivity to move might seem to have been habitual, but invariably circumstance had forced him to do so. Whilst country life was cheaper and the family benefited from the fresh air, it could not provide the access to libraries, the opportunities nor the mental stimulation the expensive city environment offered. His medical practices had rarely provided him with sufficient income to support himself and his large family and when they did, his insistence on preparing his own medicines and his radical writings brought such vicious attacks on him from the doctors and apothecaries that it became impossible, and sometimes illegal, for him to continue his practice. In any event, Hahnemann himself was unrepentant.

> They could just as well blame me for the frequent changes of my residence, as they could any other traveller. . . . Whether a man wear a round wig or a plait instead of the usual 'Swedish' head, whether he wear boots or shoes, what has it to do with them—only a man of feeble intellect would take exception. To whom do I owe anything if I go elsewhere? Let him come forward whom I have cheated out of a penny. Who gives me the money for the journey that he should have the right to ask me where I am going?

It was Alice Meynell (1847-1922) who wrote:

> Know that the mournful plain where thou must wander
> Is but a grey and silent world, but ponder
> The misty mountains of the morning yonder.

For Hahnemann, these mountains were not far away.

6.
BATTLES OF LEIPZIG
(1805-1835)

Truth for which all the eager world is fain,
Which makes us happy, lies for evermore
Not buried deep but lightly covered o'er,
By the wise hand that destined it for men.

Gellert

The Hahnemann family soon settled happily in Torgau. With his reputation growing steadily, Hahnemann's medical practice was quickly established. Henrietta married and left for Dresdorf, and Friedrich, after some differences of opinion with his parents, left home to study medicine at Leipzig. The younger children, Caroline and Frederika, were enrolled in local schools to catch up on their interrupted education, and the elder children, Wilhelmina and Amalie helped their mother with the domestic chores. Johanna, who was 41 years old, gave birth to their seventh daughter, Charlotte, later that year. It was a difficult confinement, and Charlotte was born with a very nervous disposition which was to affect her considerably in her adult life.

Dr Johann Stapf (1844) quoted a letter written by Hahnemann on his wife's confinement.

> I, for my part, look upon every increase in my family and every confinement of my wife, as one of the most important events of my life. An offshoot, composed in equal parts from me and the one who is so closely connected with me, a new being, issuing from our blood, sees the light of day, to increase the joys (and sufferings) of its parents. . . . The mother is wrestling between life and death, undecided whether she will have to give up her early existence on its account, and make her other children orphans, and be parted from the anxious husband. I see yawning before me the grave of

her who is usually so full of life, now affected to the point of death.
. . . In these hours I have always vowed to cultivate simplicity,
honesty and truth, and to find contentment and happiness in the
eyes of the Great Father of all life, on the one hand by perfecting
the innermost growth of the soul, and on the other hand, by
making those around me happy. . . . In this way I have created for
myself, during these heartrending hours, an inner life, such as we
need for eternal survival . . . and to enter calmly and cheerfully
into the reign of the all-loving, the reign of truth, vision and peace.

With the birth of yet another daughter, Louise, a little more
than a year later, the Hahnemann family was complete.

About the time that Hahnemann's elder sister, Charlotta,
received the news of the birth of her namesake in a letter from
him, Napoleon learned of his first serious setback with the news of
Nelson's total defeat of the combined French and Spanish fleets
off Cape Trafalgar on 21 October 1805, thus confirming Britain's
maritime superiority.

Hahnemann resumed his writings, which he continued
throughout his entire stay in Torgau. In 1806 he completed his
last translation, *The Materia Medica of German Plants, Together
with their Economic and Technical Use*, by Albrecht von Haller,
from the French into German. His improving financial position
now left him free to concentrate on his own original writings, and
this resulted in the publication of nineteen books and essays
between 1805 and 1811, culminating in the first edition of his
greatest work, *Organon of Rational Medicine*. Other works
published during this period included, in the chemical and pharmaceutical field: 'Substitutes for Cinchona' (Hufeland's Journal,
1806), 'What are Poisons? What are Medicines?' (Hufeland's
Journal, 1806), 'Substitutes for Foreign Drugs' (*Allegemeine
Anzeiger der Deutschen*, 1808). In the medical field he produced:
Aesculapius in the Balance (Leipzig, 1805), 'Medicine of
Experience' (Hufeland's Journal, 1806), an essay which was the
precursor to, and later altered and incorporated in, the *Organon*,
'Indications of the Homoeopathic Employment of Medicines in
Ordinary Practice' (Hufeland's Journal, 1807), 'Observations on
Scarlet Fever' (*Allegemeine Anzeiger der Deutschen*, 1808), and
another important work, *Materia Medica Pura*, Part I (Dresden,
1811).

In 1805, he published a very important book in Leipzig entitled *Fragmenta di viribus Medicamentorum positivus sive in sano corpore humano observatis*. The book was in two parts: Part I listed the symptoms produced by drugs on the healthy body and Part II listed twenty-six remedies. The remedies included *Aconite* (Monkshood), *Arnica* (Leopard's Bane), *Belladonna* (Deadly Nightshade), *Chamomilla* (Chamomile), *Drosera* (Sun Dew), *Ignatia* (St Ignatius Bean), *Ipecacuanha*, *Nux vomica* (Poison Nut) and *Pulsatilla* (Windflower), which are among the homoeopathic remedies still most widely used in the present day.

For some years Hahnemann, assisted by his wife and daughters and a few friends had been collecting plant specimens from the nearby fields and distant mountains, just as he had done as a child in the Meissen area. This time his purpose was to collect sufficient data to test clinically his hypothesis—'let likes be treated by likes' —by which remedies that have the power to create a symptom picture in the healthy body could be used to treat the same symptoms presented by the sick person. Hahnemann now revealed himself as the pragmatic experimentalist (Jenkins, 1980). Patiently and methodically he tested alcoholic extracts of the plants on himself, carefully noting the symptoms they produced, as he had done with *Cinchona* when, in his translation of Cullen's *Materia Medica* in 1790, he recorded the effects of the medicine administered to a healthy person. These tests later became known as 'provings'.

In 1810, Arnold of Dresden published the first edition of Hahnemann's *Organon der Rationellen Heilkunde* (Organon of Rational Healing), a title he later changed to *Organon of the Healing Art*. This was Hahnemann's quintessential work, a complete exposition of the new therapy. The *Organon* ran to five German editions in his lifetime and a sixth after his death, and it was subsequently translated into English, French, Italian, Spanish, Dutch, Polish, Russian, Danish, Swedish and Greek. It embraced the results of twenty years of arduous, often dangerous experimentation and observation. The principle *similia similibus*, enunciated in his essay of 1796, was now expanded to *similia similibus curentor*—'Let likes be treated with likes'—the essential basic principle of homoeopathy.

The author's preface of the *Organon* quoted the lines of Gellert, Hahnemann's fellow pupil at The Prince's School in Meissen, which introduce this chapter. In later editions, this poem was replaced by the motto of The Prince's School—'Aude Sapere'.

In his preface to the book, Hahnemann wrote:

> Through my enquiry into the art of healing I found the road to truth upon which I have to tread alone, a road far removed from the common highway of medical routine. The further I advanced from truth to truth, the further did my conclusion move from the traditional approach, built only on opinion, although I allowed no single one of my conclusions to stand unless fully confirmed by experiment.
>
> The results of these convictions are stated in this book. It remains to be seen whether physicians who intend to deal fairly with their consciences and with humanity can open their eyes to the health-giving truth.
>
> This warning at least I would give at the beginning, that indolence, desire for ease and obstinacy make service at the altar of truth impossible, and that only freedom from prejudice and tireless zeal avail for the most holy of the endeavours of mankind, the practice of the true art of healing. But the physician who works in this spirit follows close after God, the Creator of the world, whose creatures he helps to uphold.

The first two paragraphs of the book read as follows:

1. The physician has no higher aim than to make sick people well, to pursue what is called the Art of Healing.
2. The highest ideal of cure is the speedy, gentle and enduring restoration of health, or the removal and annihilation of disease in its entirety by the quickest, most trustworthy, and least harmful way according to principles that can be readily understood.

The new principles of homoeopathic medicine were set out in 271 paragraphs (increasing to 291 paragraphs in the sixth edition). Apart from stating the basic principle of homoeopathy, he described his experimentation with different strengths of remedies. He was well aware that some of the remedies in their most concentrated form were highly poisonous and he had, therefore, successively reduced the size of the dose. Experimenting in this way he found that not only was the effectiveness maintained, but even increased, when the dose was infinitesimally small. He achieved this by a process of serial (or sequential) dilution of the alcoholic extract of the macerated plant material, or *mother tincture*. The number of dilutions determined the *potency* (although Hahnemann did not use this term until later editions of the *Organon*). Thus, the first *decimal* potency (1x) consisted of one part of mother tincture and nine parts of an alcohol-water mixture. One part of potency 1x added to a further nine of the alcohol-water mixture gave a potency of 2x, and so on. The so-called *centesimal* series of potencies were produced by adding 99 parts of the alcohol-water mixture to 1 part of the mother tincture for the first potency (1c), nd so on. After each dilution in either series the solution was *succussed*, that is shaken vigorously with impact. The impact was achieved by Hahnemann by banging the vial containing the solution several times on a leather bound book, but nowadays this is achieved by mechanical means.

The third principle of homoeopathy related to the prescribing of homoeopathic medicines. The physician prescribes individually by the study of the whole person according to their basic temperament and responses. Consequently he must diagnose the patient as a whole and not just make a physical diagnosis. He must consider, for example, whether the patient prefers to be alone or in company, whether the patient is artistic or practical, or does he or she prefer hot or cold weather. These are valuable pointers to the selection of the remedies. This is because the original provings of the drugs, the changes produced by these drugs in healthy people were noted not only on the physical body of the prover, but also on his or her mental, emotional or climatic conditions. It is for this reason that different homoeopathic medicines may be prescribed for different people for the same disease. Finally, Hahnemann made a controversial statement that only one single medicine should be given to the patient at one time and the use of mixtures was inadmissible.

The sixth and last edition of the *Organon* was not published until 1922. It was a thoroughly revised version of the fifth edition, annotated and changed in Hahnemann's own handwriting, paragraph by paragraph in the light of his experience in the latter part of his career in the treatment of both acute and chronic diseases. William Boericke, to whom we are indebted for the rescue of the manuscript and the English translation, wrote: 'Historically, the sixth edition is one of the greatest importance, completing the marvellous array of Hahnemann's philosophic insight into the practice of medicine.' Of greatest importance were additional paragraphs relating to dosage in the treatment of chronic diseases, where he advised repetition of doses, but in different potencies. He also added four further paragraphs on the details of the preparation of homoeopathic medicines.

Bradford (1895) reported that the publication of the *Organon* led to violent warfare against Hahnemann when he was called, *inter alia*, a charlatan, a quack and an ignoramus, but all the evidence suggests that it was received with only mild interest and very little positive reaction, favourable or otherwise. One reviewer stated that there might be some value in homoeopathy for certain individual cases, and another stated that, although it was too general, he was not altogether dissatisfied with its contents. What criticism there was centred largely on the size of the dose, which was considered too small to be effective. To Hahnemann, who, from his previous experience, had expected an outcry, the comparative silence was deafening. He wrote only one reply to all criticisms, in an effort to provoke *some* reaction to his book, in *Der Reichanzeiger* in 1811:

> Is it really credible that, in these illumined times, a work of exper-
> ience like my *Organon of Rational Healing*, springing purely from
> experience, referable only to experience and confirmable or
> refutable only by counter-experience and counter-experiments,
> was put to one side by several reviewers with empty words and
> expressions?

An attack which Bradford described as 'especially bitter' did appear in an article written by a Dr A. F. Hecker and published in *Annalen der Gesammten Medicin*, and a refutation was published in a pamphlet by Hahnemann's son Friedrich, who was then a student at Leipzig University. It was suggested by Dudgeon, how-ever, that Hahnemann himself, and not his son, wrote the refu-tation as it was written in his own style, probably dictated to Friedrich.

Meanwhile the Peninsular War was sapping Napoleon's power, with more than a quarter of a million troops locked up in Spain fighting off the thrusts of the army of General Arthur Wellesley (later the Duke of Wellington). In spite of this, his plans for conquest in Eastern Europe went forward, which was to cause Saxony to gravitate inexorably towards the centre of world events. During the winter of 1810-1811, Napoleon built a defensive line along the Elbe, from Hamburg in the north to Dresden in the south, to keep the way open to Danzig where his troops were cut off, and to Russia. Napoleon himself took up an entrenched position outside Dresden and his ablest marshal, Davout, fortified Hamburg. Magdeburg, halfway between, was turned into formidable fortress and intermediate fortresses were built at the main river crossings. Torgau was heavily fortified, with its ramparts protecting the bridge—the same bridge which was again to become the centre of world events when American and Russian soldiers linked hands in April 1945. Large fleets of barges loaded with stone and building materials were moored to the banks of the Elbe and large numbers of French troops set up encampments just outside the town.

These events clearly unsettled Hahnemann. He wrote to a friend, Dr von Villers,

Torgau, 30 January 1811

I am now nearly fifty years old, surrounded by my family which is very dear to me—a wife of exceptional kindness and seven happy, almost grown up daughters, who are well educated, obedient and innocent. They take care of me and brighten my life (also with music). I am nearly always able to heal quickly and permanently any patients entrusted to my care. . . . Am I not to be envied? But see, they are making all preparations to transmute Torgau into a big and terrible fortress, in which my family is not likely to live in peace. I have to sell my dear and comfortable freehold house and move—undecided—where?

Further correspondence between Hahnemann and von Villers, who was a lecturer at the University of Göttingen, indicated that he toyed with the idea of returning to that town, where he had stayed briefly seventeen years before, during his travels. Subsequent events showed that he tried to obtain a similar position as a lecturer at the University, but when he failed, he decided to move to Leipzig instead.

He wrote to his favourite sister, Charlotta, who had now re-married a Dr Muller of Eisleben after the death of her first husband, informing her of his intention to move to Leipzig. She replied as follows on 18 June 1811:

> My Dear Brother, ˙
> Oh, how much I would like to press you and yours once more to my heart in this life! I would have travelled the world to have done it, but unfortunately your news makes it impossible. . . . May Leipzig be the scene of all the earthly happiness that it is possible for you to enjoy in this world. Alas, dear brother, I cannot tell you all that my soul would express,
>
> > Your Loving Sister,
> > Charlotte Muller

On 3 December 1811, he wrote to his old friend, Councillor Becker, 'I believe you do know that I am six miles nearer to you. I was threatened to be swallowed up amidst the gigantic ramparts of Torgau and I escaped here to Leipzig. But I do regret the pretty house I have left and the garden round it, where I think I have puzzled out many things for the good of man.'

At the beginning of September, he had moved to a house at 147 in the distinguished Burgstrasse in Leipzig, called *Die Goldene Fahne* or 'The Golden Flag' (Humpert reported 'The Golden Banner'). Bearing in mind his reasons for leaving Torgau, it might have been better for him and his family if he had secured the post in Göttingen, for Leipzig and not Torgau was shortly to become the venue for one of the most decisive battles of the Napoleonic Wars. Other events, which chequered his career, were to cause him to regret his choice of Leipzig.

The cultural and academic environment of Leipzig had always appealed to Hahnemann, although his previous periods in the city had not been particularly happy. This was the fourth time he had come; the first time as a homesick grocery assistant, the second as an impecunious and uncertain university student and the third, in 1789, as a struggling physician.

Undeterred by the lukewarm and largely apathetic reception of his new doctrine, Hahnemann attempted to set up an Institute for the Postgraduate Study of Homoeopathy. His announcement of this venture appeared in *Der Reichanzeiger* on 4 December 1811.

Medical Institute

I feel that my doctrine enunciated in the *Organon of Rational Healing* aroused the highest expectations for the welfare of the sick. But by its very nature it is so new and striking and opposes almost all medical dogmas and traditional observations, that it cannot so readily gain acceptance among the otherwise educated physicians unless practical demonstration comes to its assistance. In order to effect this object, and thus to show them that the homoeopathic method of healing, new as it is, is the only acceptable, the most consistent, the simplest and the surest way of healing human disease, I have decided to open here in Leipzig, at the beginning of April, an Institute for Graduate Physicians . . . a six month tutorial course on the theory and practice of homoeopathy will be sufficient to grasp the principles of this most helpful science of healing. More detailed conditions will be sent on receipt of a prepaid envelope.

Dr Samuel Hahnemann

Not a single doctor applied for the course. Undismayed, he promptly applied to the Dean of the Faculty of Medicine at the University of Leipzig for permission to give medical lectures. On 10 February the Dean replied that an external doctor, although qualified to practise, was not allowed to deliver lectures until he had defended his own dissertation from the Upper Chair with a respondent and deposited 50 talers (about £20) with the Faculty. Hahnemann took up the challenge, and on 26 June the following year, at nearly sixty years of age, he delivered the required speech in Latin to a capacity audience in the Grand Auditorium in a masterly style of oratory.

The subject of his 86-page thesis was the historical-medical aspects of treatment and cure with White Hellebore, (the much used medicine *Veratrum album*, which he proved was the *Helleborus* used in the first century A.D.).

He was able to quote verbatim from many publications in eight different languages, thus impressing the audience with his extraordinary ability for languages and his scholastic knowledge, particularly in the history of medicine. Tactfully, he avoided any reference to homoeopathy or anything which might be considered to be contentious. It is not surprising, therefore, that his speech was well received and even the Dean, Professor Ludwig, commented favourably. One reviewer described the dissertation as 'an interesting contribution to the history of medical science' and another, 'a very thorough essay'. A Dr Huck of Lutzen, near Leipzig, who was present that day, wrote on 9 August:

> To hear Hahnemann, the keenest and boldest investigator of nature, deliver a masterly piece of his intellect and industry, was to me a truly beatific enjoyment. . . . The strongest of his opponents were so courteous as to acknowledge that they were wholly of his opinion, medically speaking. . . . He covered himself with renown —he remained victor. Had it not been an unsuitable time of day, I would have gone to him and should have voluntarily and unconditionally taken myself to his banner.

(He subsequently christened his son, Luther Hahnemann Huck.)

Hahnemann opened his course of lectures at the commencement of the new academic year in the Winter Term on 29 September 1812, with two lectures a week on Wednesday and Saturday at 2 p.m.

In the same month, the Grand Army, the mightiest Napoleon had yet commanded, having launched its attack on Russia the previous year, began its celebrated retreat from Moscow. The disastrous retreat over devastated ground, in the grip of the cold of the Russian winter and pursued by the enemy, inflicted hideous losses, and encouraged Prussia and Austria to declare war against France. Napoleon immediately raised new armies, drawing heavily on his army in Spain, and in August 1813 he was back in Saxony with 160,000 men, where he won a great victory over the Allied armies at Dresden. Moving north-west to Leipzig, he re-engaged the Allied army, now 240,000 strong, and commanded by Field Marshal Prince Karl of Schwarzenburg, in the Battle of Leipzig or the 'Battle of the Nations' (Volkerschlacht).

Napoleon, accompanied by his uncertain ally Friedrich, King of Saxony, arrived at Leipzig on 14 October 1813 and took up his quarters just outside the city. During August and September weary troops had poured into the city. The streets were choked with refugees, horses and carts, cannons and troop transports and herds of cattle which had been driven into the city for safety.

The incessant autumn rain rendered the roads impassable. Food supplies dwindled daily, and the shops were besieged before the streets finally emptied and a curfew was imposed from dusk until dawn. Like most of the city's inhabitants, Hahnemann and his family would have gathered together a supply of food and water and taken refuge in their cellars. During the nights of 16 and 17 October the yellow-orange glow of burning villages illuminated the sky to the north and west of the city, and the intermittent roar of the cannons made sleep impossible. Young Charlotte and Louise who were very nervous, would have suffered much distress and they would certainly have needed constant comfort and reassurance from their parents.

The battle reached its height on 18 October. The noise of explosions, the roar of cannons, the shouts of soldiers and the screams of the wounded and terrified inhabitants rose to a crescendo as bullets spattered the walls of houses. On 19 October seventeen Saxon regiments suddenly turned on Napoleon, tipping the scales against him. A fire broke out on the Brühl, while hordes of retreating French soldiers blocked the Ranstadt Gate. Shortly before midday a tremendous explosion rocked the whole city as the bridge was blown up. The city gates were stormed by the Allied troops and, with Napoleon's army decisively defeated and King Friedrich and his family captured, Prince Karl of Schwarzenburg led a column through the streets to the strains of music and the sound of bells. Napoleon retreated from Germany and never returned; the whole of Hahnemann's beloved Saxony was at peace for the first time in his life! When Hahnemann's path crossed with Prince Karl of Schwarzenburg again, it was to result in traumatic consequences for him.

During the next few days, along with the field surgeons and other doctors from the Faculty of Medicine, led by a Dr Griesslich, Hahnemann did what he could to alleviate the terrible suffering of the hundreds of maimed and dying soldiers and civilians who filled the military hospital, which had been hastily set up in the University Church, to overflowing. The magnitude of the task may be seen in the light of the fact that the holocaust had resulted in 80,000 men killed and the same number wounded on the battlefield, in only three days. Ironically, the aftermath of the battle brought with it the opportunity for Hahnemann to establish homoeopathy as a real alternative to the medical practices then existent. Polluted drinking water brought a new peril to the city—an outbreak of typhus which caused a mounting death toll. Hahnemann treated all his patients homoeopathically and achieved remarkable success in comparison with the results of the conventional treatment. This was the first public demonstration of the efficacy of homoeopathic therapy and word of its success began to spread far beyond Saxony. His experiences were published a year later, in 1814, in *Allegemeine Anzeige der Deutschen*, under the title, 'Treatment of the Now Prevailing Typhus Fever'. He recorded that, of 180 patients treated, only two died (and one of these a very old man) and he gave an account of his success with two homoeopathic medicines.

Hahnemann had not had an article published in *Allegemeine Anzeige der Deutschen* for more than two years, as this newspaper had been banned from publication for seventeen months during 1812 and 1813. His loyal and courageous friend, Councillor Becker of Gotha, had always been ready to publish Hahnemann's most controversial medical articles, but his own political articles brought him into conflict with the Government. At that time, Germany was a loose confederation of small autonomous States and Principalities, and Councillor Becker's campaign for greater unity resulted in the suspension of his newspaper and his own imprisonment for 'expressing sentiments of German patriotism'. He resumed publication of his newspaper on his release in 1813.

Napoleon's defeat at Waterloo in June 1815 by the Allied Armies commanded by the Duke of Wellington, finally brought peace to the whole of Europe and with increasing prosperity, the social life and cultural activities of Leipzig flourished.

Many years later, the Duke of Wellington developed some interest in homoeopathy. *The British Homoeopathic Journal* (October 1974) reported a letter the Duke wrote, in September

1842, to the daughter of the Earl of Derby, that he had read Dr Curie's (grandfather of Marie Curie, discoverer of radium) book and he was impressed with the principles of homoeopathy and the extent of the experiments carried out. He went on to urge that trials should be carried out, under his friend's patronage, in an English hospital to test these principles. There is no record that his proposal was acted upon.

As life in Leipzig returned to normal Hahnemann resumed his biweekly lectures at the University. When he had begun a year earlier his lectures attracted high attendances, but after a calm, eloquent beginning when he expounded the positive features of homoeopathy, his lectures habitually degenerated into a negative, uncontrolled and abusive attack on contemporary medicine and those who practised it, to the point when he became almost incoherent and lost the sympathy of his audiences. Haehl (1922) related that after reading a paragraph from his *Organon*, Hahnemann's professional calm and dignity promptly disappeared when he broke out into 'a raging hurricane'. Dr Franz Hartmann, one of his most faithful students and followers, and therefore not one to readily criticize him, wrote sadly:

> Unfortunately the lectures were not fitted to win friends and followers for his theories or himself. For whenever possible, he poured forth a flood of abuse against the older medicine and its followers, with the result that his audience lessened every hour and finally consisted of only a few of his students. And others were present, not for the subject matter, but to hear the unfortunate method of presentation, so that their sense of humour might be freely tickled.

Rosa Hobhouse (1933) was of the opinion that this may have been a blessing in disguise, in that his attitude ensured that the few followers he did gather round him were wholehearted supporters. Ruthven Mitchell (1975) did not accept this view, reasoning that Hahnemann's unrestrained and needlessly insulting attacks not only repelled the half-hearted but also embarrassed and strained the loyalty of the faithful. He went on to suggest that his new homoeopathy might have gained a great deal if Hahnemann had sought best of the old—a view which is relevant, even with the situation as it exists today. Undoubtedly, years of professional isolation and conflict had resulted in Hahnemann being over-sensitive to criticism and ready to take a defensive stance at the slightest provocation. From later accounts, it is evident that much of this provocation was deliberate on the part of some mischievous students who were quick to recognize his vulnerability.

We are indebted to Franz Hartmann's revealing insight into Hahnemann's lifestyle in Leipzig, in a series of articles published in *Allegemeine Hom. Zeitung* between 1844 and 1850. Hartmann entered Leipzig University in 1814 at the age of eighteen and was introduced to Hahnemann by an exceptionally brilliant student, Karl Hornburg. He soon became a disciple of Hahnemann and his new therapy and developed a lasting friendship with him. Hahnemann's eccentric behaviour in the lecture room was described by Hartmann as follows:

> He presented, from his arrival to his departure from the lecture room such a peculiar appearance that it would have taken men of his own type of mind and age to look seriously into his eyes; for young minds and cheery students who are easily stimulated to laughter at the slightest provocation it would have been impossible to demand a serious demeanour.
>
> However imposing and commanding of respect, Hahnemann's external appearance was, in his simple study, with his upright carriage, his firm step, his plain way of dressing, just as much was his appearance grotesque for this one hour: even he seemed to enjoy himself, and was trying to draw attention in a genial way. Think of the tension of the audience before his arrival, who as yet did not know the enthusiastic reformer, or perhaps were rubbing their hands in joyous anticipation of the volcanic eruptions—and you will tender forgiveness for the smile, when you hear the outer door open and hear his step in the adjacent room, where he remains standing at the door, clears his throat, and then turns the key round twice in the lock; the door which is usually locked is seen to open, and a man enters of middle height and strong build; the few hairs of the thoughtful head are carefully curled and powdered, inspiring respect for his advanced age, which would have been apparent even if the bald crown and white hair had not been powdered; add to that the beautiful white linen round the neck and on the chest. The black waistcoat and the short black

trousers; on the button of the latter was fastened the strap of his shining black top boots, above which appeared the finest white stockings. Think of this figure as, after three measured steps, he gives an almost imperceptible nod of the head as a sign of greeting, then takes three more steps and having arrived at his chair, in front of which is a little table, he sits down with pathos after removing carefully the shining tails of his coat, opens the book, takes out his watch and puts it on the table before him, then clears his throat, reads the respective paragraph with ordinary voice, but becomes more ecstatic during his explanations, with shining and sparkling eyes, and great redness of the forehead and face—I ask how could it be possible to keep a serious face in young years when one is inclined to ridicule everything and not even spare old age.

This account cannot be taken too seriously, however, for generations of students have made the age and eccentricity of their tutors the butt for their youthful high spirits, whilst respecting their academic brilliance. Hahnemann continued his lecturing well into his sixties, which was considered to be very old in an age when the average lifespan was little more than forty-five years.

In spite of his shortcomings in the lecture room, Hahnemann was gathering around him a small, but enthusiastic and talented group of supporters, who followed him and his teachings with a missionary zeal. His disciples were mainly young students, as the qualified doctors seemed too prejudiced through their conventional training to accept the new concepts of homoeopathy. Hartmann wrote:

> We lived very happily together, caring little for the hostile glances and remarks of our colleagues. We stuck to our studies faithfully and honestly and gathered together occasionally in our teacher Hahnemann's household some time after eight in the evening. By this we felt invigorated against new attacks, for Hahnemann was very skilful in stimulating anew our depressed spirits.

Hahnemann's own sentiments were prosaically expressed in a letter to his close friend and disciple, Dr Stapf:

Leipzig, September 1815

At present homoeopathy grows with slow progress amid the

abundance of weeds which luxuriate about it. It grows unobserved, from an unlikely acorn into a little plant; soon may its head be seen overtopping the tall weeds. Be patient—it is striking its roots deep into the earth:it is strengthening itself unperceived but all the more certainly in its own time it will increase, till it becomes an oak of God, whose arms stretch that the suffering children of men may be revived under its benificent shadow.

Hahnemann's domestic and professional life at his home in No. 147 Burgstrasse, surrounded by his family and his medical colleagues, settled into a most agreeable and well ordered routine.

In'1817, he even resumed his Masonic activities, which he had allowed to lapse since he left Hermannstadt for Erlangen in 1779, by joining the Leipzig Lodge, 'Minerva of the Three Palms'.

The surgery hours for his flourishing practice were from 9 a.m. until 12 noon Mondays to Saturdays and from 2 p.m. until 4 p.m., Mondays to Fridays, except for Wednesdays, when he gave his lectures at the University. On successive weeks, his daughters, Caroline, Frederika and Eleonore, would act as receptionists, sitting by a small window by the hall door. The hall was usually filled with waiting patients, whilst Hahnemann gave full consultations, examining his patients systematically and accurately, entering the symptoms himself in his notebook. The patients collected their medicines in an adjoining room and were shown out of the house by one of his daughters. Promptly at 12 noon he would be called to lunch. Hartmann recorded that, once when he ignored Johanna's call to lunch for a second time, Hahnemann remarked, 'This time I shall get a black look.'

When the surgery closed in the afternoon, it was Hahnemann's custom to take his family for a walk for about an hour. The Hahnemann family taking their daily walk along the main promenade by the city wall, or sometimes on a longer walk to neighbouring Schleuzig Küchengarten or Gohlis, was a familiar sight. He would walk alongside Johanna in a dignified fashion, dressed in a dark coat, short tight trousers and white silk stockings with leather, buckled shoes and carrying a three cornered hat. He was followed dutifully by his well disciplined daughters, dressed in stiff corsets with hooped, ankle length dresses and wearing bonnets edged with frilled lace. Like all young German ladies at this time, their dress followed the French style as much as possible, for Paris had already established itself as the centre of world fashion. Ernst von Brunnow, a young law student, who later befriended Hahnemann, embellished the scene when he wrote:

> It was a clear spring day in 1816 when I sauntered with my companions along the cheerful promenade of Leipzig. Among the teachers from the University were to be found at that time many notables. Many a professor stalked gravely along in old-fashioned dress of the previous century with peruque and bag, silk stockings and buckles on his shoes, while the pampered sons of the landed gentry swaggered about in hussar jackets and pantaloons orna-mented with points, or in leather breeches with high dragoon boots and clinking spurs. The celebrated Dr Hahnemann, the old gentleman with an extraordinarily intelligent countenance, walks respectfully arm in arm with his somewhat corpulent wife and followed by his two pairs of rosy daughters. He is the discoverer of the homoeopathic system of medicine which is turning conventional medicine topsy turvy.

In the evenings, Hahnemann often invited groups of his friends and students to his home for family gatherings, where he kept everyone entertained with his wit and his conversation. Hartmann described these occasions in 1844 from his own experience:

> There sat the silver-haired old man, with his high arched, thoughtful brow, his bright, piercing eyes, and calm searching countenance, in the midst of us, as among his children, who like-wise participated in those evening entertainments. Here he showed plainly that the serious exterior which he exhibited in everyday life, belonged only to his deep and constant search after the goal which he had set himself, but was in no respect the mirror of his interior, the bright side of which so readily unfolded itself on suitable occasions in its fairest light, and the mirthful humour, the familiarity and openness, the wit that he displayed were alike engaging.
>
> How comfortable the master felt in the circle of his beloved and his friends, among whom he numbered not only his pupils but also the learned of other faculties, who did homage to his learning;

how beneficial was the recreation which he then allowed himself after eight o'clock in the evening, seated in his armchair wearing his velvet cap and dressing gown, with a glass of light Leipzig white beer and his pipe. It was highly interesting at such times to see him become cheerful, as he related the procedure of the older physicians at the sick bed, when with an animated countenance he moved the little cap to and fro upon his head, and puffed out clouds of tobacco smoke, which enveloped him like a fog; when he spoke of his deeply affecting life and related circumstances of it, his pipe often went out, and one of his daughters was then instantly required to light it again. He liked to converse especially on objects of the natural sciences or on conditions of foreign countries and their inhabitants, and he appeared displeased when in these hours his advice was sought in cases of disease. He was then either laconic, or called out to the patient in a friendly way 'tomorrow on this subject', not in order to put the matter aside, but because he was too tired to speak on serious subjects, for often he would refer to the question raised, during his consulting hours on the following day, and stood by with his kind advice. He liked to see people express their opinion openly, even if they contradicted him, and occasionally he would surrender his opinion to that of his opponent.

Perhaps the suppers which were given once or twice a year by Hahnemann to his pupils formed a suitable means of bringing a little change into this monotonous way of living, but he never invited any but those who distinguished themselves through diligence, intelligence and strict morality. During these supper parties things were not altogether homoeopathic, for although I can vouch for a perfect simplicity of the food served, yet instead of white beer, a good wine was provided, of which, however, out of deference to the Master only a moderate amount was consumed. At these entertainments Hahnemann, on the one side and his wife on the other, separated his family from the guests (five daughters—his son and two married daughters were no longer at home). Joyous humour and wit dominated these gatherings, and the desire to laugh was unending, for as a rule other talented men were invited. Here Hahnemann was the most cheerful man, even entering into the pranks of the others, yet without offending propriety, or making any one present the target of his jokes. When the meal was ended a pipe was smoked, and about 11 o'clock we took our leave and banqueted long after on the recollections of those delightful evenings.

Again, von Brunnow added his own impressions of Hahnemann's lifestyle:

> Hahnemann at that time was in his sixty-second year. Locks of silver white hair clustered round his high and thoughtful brow, from under which his animated eyes shone with piercing brilliancy. His whole countenance had a quiet, searching, grand expression. . . . His carriage was upright, his step firm, his motions as lively as a man of thirty. When he was out his dress was of the simplest; a dark coat with short small clothes and stockings. But in his room he preferred the old household; gaily figured dressing gown, the yellow stockings and the black velvet cap. The long pipe was seldom out of his hand, and the smoking was the only infringement he allowed himself to commit upon his severe routine. His drink was water, milk or beer; his food was of the most frugal sort. The whole of his domestic economy was as simple as his food and dress. Instead of a writing desk he used nothing but a large plain deal table.

Von Brunnow added that, 'Hahnemann had a liking for the Chinese, and his favourite topics for conversation were the natural sciences and conditions in other countries. He was a pure Deist, but with complete conviction.'

The influence of Hahnemann's late father was evident in the strict obedience, frugality, industry and diligence he demanded from his daughters. Even though, in the early nineteenth century in Germany, some were already deploring the lack of respect children showed for their parents, Hahnemann held to the traditional standards. Generally, girls counted little in comparison with the opportunities afforded to boys and, in most families, little or no effort was made to educate them. Daughters were expected to share the daily work in the household, and afterwards there was a choice between spinning and weaving, knitting or embroidery. Long before marriage, therefore, their trousseaux were ready, which was expected when matches were made for them.

Hahnemann undertook most of his daughters' education himself, whilst Johanna taught them music on their rather old piano. Hahnemann taught them French, since a knowledge of French, and keeping abreast of French fashion and etiquette, was considered an essential part of the education of a young lady. A German manual of this period on the education of daughters stated: 'To talk German is only for the daughters of laymen and for spinsters; young ladies on the other hand must be able to say "Bon Jour" or "Je vous souhaite une bonne nuit".'

His daughters feminine interest in fashion was not shared by their father, who had a particular aversion to the wearing of stays, corsets and garters, which he held to be the cause of varicose veins, constipation and fainting fits. He often held forth on this subject, but, for his daughters at least, his advice fell on deaf ears.

As previously described, Hahnemann's eldest daughters, Caroline, Frederika and Eleonore, (now in their thirties) also assisted their father in his medical practice, whilst the youngest daughters, Charlotte and Louise (now in their teens), who were extremely shy and nervous, rarely left the house, apart from their walks with their parents. It is clear that all eight daughters demonstrated their love and respect for their parents throughout their lives and theirs was an austere, yet, happy, home.

Of great significance to the development of homoeopathy was Hahnemann's decision to form a group of collaborators for the *proving* of new medicines. These medicines might then be added to the original twenty-six remedies which had been the subject of his earlier provings during his stay in Torgau. This 'Provers Union', as earlier biographers have described it, consisted of healthy volunteers who were prepared to subject themselves to the testing of drugs on themselves and record the symptoms they produced, regardless of the dangers involved. The original provers were Drs Stapf, Hartmann, Gross, Hornburg, Franz, Wislicenus, Teuthorn, Herrmann, Laughammer, E. Ruckert and L. Ruckert, Hahnemann himself, Johanna, and their daughters, Caroline and Frederika. Later, other provers were recruited, including Hahnemann's son Friedrich, his son-in-law, Dr Theodore Mossdorf, and Drs Becker, Harnisch, Meyer, Wagner, Wenzel, Caspan, Gunther, Urban and Adam (a Russian physician).

The accuracy of this research was ensured by the strict procedures laid down by Hahnemann. The medicines were provided by him in the form of an essence or tincture of the first or second potency and he always told the prover the source of the medicine. Since he invariably tried the drugs on himself, he had sufficient knowledge to prescribe the appropriate strength. He took great pains to reduce the risk to the prover to the minimum by developing antidotes. Thus, in a letter to Dr Stapf, his instructions were as follows:

> When I propose anything for proving, I take care that it is nothing which will ruin health. . . . I enclose some tincture of *Helleborus niger*, which I gathered myself. Each grain contains one twentieth grain of the root. . . . Take one drop to eight ounces of water and a scruple of alcohol (to prevent decomposition) shake it briskly and take one ounce before breakfast and every 1 ½ to 2 hours thereafter as long as you are not too severely affected. Should severe symptoms occur, take some drops of tincture of Camphor in one ounce of water, or more if necessary, as this will allay the symptoms.

He required the prover to avoid any extraneous influences which may have distorted the results. During a proving he would forbid the use of coffee or tea, wine or brandy, spices or strongly salted foods, but not beer, and he did not encourage any games or work activity which might disturb the concentration or judgement of the prover. He did advise moderate exercise, however. The prover was required to write down every dose, every symptom and the time of each event. Finally, Hahnemann, would, as he explained to Dr Stapf, 'go through the symptoms along with them, asking questions so as to complete from their recollections that which requires to be more explicit.' Many years later, Hahnemann wrote:

> On every occasion when my Leipzig colleagues delivered their essays on provings I questioned them in respect of the symptoms they observed in order to get as precisely as possible the verbal expressions of their sensations and sufferings and to ascertain exactly the conditions under which the symptoms occurred. I also knew that they had observed the carefully regulated diet during their provings.

Over the years the procedures became so refined that the proving of medicines became an art (or science) in its own right, and it still forms the basis of the system which is practised today.

In a tribute to the intrepid experimenters, Dr Margaret Tyler wrote in 1931, 'For years, for half a lifetime, they had been proving drug after drug and suffering their effects in their own minds and bodies. The greatest ability to help is achieved ever at the greatest cost.'

The result of this laborious, painstaking work of proving homoeopathic medicines were published in Hahnemann's *Materia Medica Pura*, in six parts between 1811 and 1821. Several thousand symptoms were recorded in an index covering sixty-six individual medicines, together with instructions for the preparation of the medicines for homoeopathic use, the historical use of each medicine and the main diseases for which each medicine might be prescribed. In some editions, Hahnemann remonstrated against conventional methods of treatment and the massive doses of medicine employed. Of particular significance was his comment on the homoeopathic approach to prescribing: '. . . it would be, therefore, the duty of the physician to distinguish the subtle variations of every *individual* case—that is to specialize and *individualize* in each personal case, instead of treating the diseases.' In another edition he concluded: '. . . only the most careful observer can become a true scientific healer.'

In the third edition, after recapitulating the doctrine of homoeopathic medicine, he defiantly concluded:

> There is no case of dynamic disease in the world whose symptoms cannot be met with the great similarity among the positive effects of a medicine, which will not be rapidly and permanently cured of this malady in no more easy, rapid, certain, reliable and permanent manner by any conceivable method of treatment other than by means of homoeopathic medicine in small doses.

In his foreword to this same edition, he reproved those who were partly converted to homoeopathy and had begged him to publish more exact directions. He pointed out that his *Organon of Rational Medicine* contained everything they required to know.

In some editions, Hahnemann remonstrated against conventional methods of treatment and the massive doses employed. In the second edition, he could not resist the temptation to reply to the inevitable criticisms of the first edition, and wrote in a style which gives a hint of his outbursts in the lecture room:

Leipzig, February 1817

I have read several unfair criticisms of the second volume of my *Materia Medica Pura*, especially my essay on the doctrine of homoeopathic medicine. Now I could easily settle them here in the traditional manner of writers and expose them in all their nakedness, but I shall not do so. I do not wish to burden myself with the sin of immortalizing these follies and their perpetrators. . . . Perversion of words and sense, which is meant to appear learned, abuse and sceptical shaking of the head, instead of practical demonstrations to the contrary are too absurd to use against the facts of homoeopathy. What ignorance my critics display—they are not even aware of the difference between *homoeopathy* [similar] and *homopathy* [same]. They remind me of mischievous boys with gunpowder—the things which fizz and splutter but are not very effective and on the whole are miserable affairs. . . . Their brains are so stuffed full of fanciful ideas, insane maxims, systems and dogmas and a load of practical trash, they are no longer capable without inhibition to practise a simple system like homoeopathy.

Clearly, Hahnemann, when criticized, gave as good as he got. In his preamble to the proving of *Aconite*, Hahnemann returned to his campaign against blood-letting:

Traditional medicine has hitherto employed copious blood-letting, often ineffectually, and almost always with disastrous consequences. I allude to the pure inflammatory fevers, where the smallest dose of *Aconite* relieves rapidly and without side-effects. . . . It is precisely in the acute inflammatory fevers in which allopathy chiefly plumes itself as alone being able to save life by bold, frequent venesections, believing it to be superior to homoeopathy. Homoeopathy need not shed a single drop of blood, that precious vital liquid which the traditional doctor recklessly draws off in streams, thus requiring months for the restoration of health of those not carried off by death in the process.

In spite of the manner of presentation being unsatisfactory in some respects, his *Materia Medica Pura* remains as a particularly important scientific study. It is significant that, over the years, large sections of this work have found their way into the standard Pharmacopoeia.

In view of his academic activities in lecturing and research, his thriving practice and his family and social life, it is not surprising that Hahnemann's writing was limited during this period of his life, particularly when one considers that he had reached an age (sixty-six in 1821) when most men would have retired. Apart from his dissertation for his acceptance as a lecturer at the University and his major work, *Materia Medica Pura*, he had several minor works published. These included his paper on the treatment of typhoid fever (in *Allegemeine Anzeige der Deutschen*, 1814); 'Venereal Disease and its Ordinary Improper Treatment' (ibid. 1816); 'The Treatment of Burns' (ibid. 1816) and 'The Preparation and Dispensing of Medicines by Homoeopathic Physicians Themselves' (1820). A literary feud in the local newspapers with a Dr Dzondi following his paper in *Allegemeine Anzeige der Deutschen* over the antiquated methods of curing burns, although spread over more than two years (from 1816 to 1818), proved to be of little consequence.

Apart from this minor feud, Hahnemann's seven years in Leipzig, until 1818, were relatively peaceful and most constructive. His practice had flourished and his reputation had grown as homoeopathy began to be practised more widely in Germany and in several other European countries and Johanna had enjoyed with him a long settled period in one home, the longest stay anywhere in their married life. But storm clouds were gathering again; a chain of events over the next two years were to result in conflict and turmoil, more traumatic than even he had previously encountered in his turbulent life.

In 1818, Hahnemann and his family mourned the death of their third child and second daughter, Wilhelmina, who had married Herr Richter, the Director of Music from Gera, and had borne a son, Hermann. She had died, aged only thirty, of an unreported cause, in Stottertiz, the suburb of Leipzig where the family had lived for a brief period when Wilhelmina was a young child.

Antagonized by thriving homoeopathic practices appearing everywhere, the first shots in a new campaign of hostility by the local doctors and apothecaries were fired in 1819. Dr J. K. Bischoff, a physician of some influence and Chief Physician of the Prague General Infirmary, published a work entitled 'Views on the Methods of Healing up to this Time and on the First Principles of Homoeopathy'. In this work he acknowledged

Hahnemann's earlier contributions to medicine and approved his provings of medicines and the method of their preparation, but he rejected Hahnemann's homoeopathic principles, preferring conventional methods 'which by reason of the industry of the physicians have such a beneficient efficacy for mankind'. He also opposed Hahnemann in his criticism of blood-letting.

Later the same year a more constructive criticism, written by a Professor Puchelt, appeared in Hufeland's Journal. In his own words, the aim of the essay was 'To criticize Hahnemann's homoeopathy, which is beginning to be more and more widespread among the younger doctors of the latest generation and is gaining a reputation with the lay public.' He attacked Hahnemann for his utter contempt for the rest of medicine and suggested that homoeopathy might have been acceptable 'had he not declared open war on the whole of the rest of medicine.' He wrote, 'However contradictory it may appear at first sight to want to cure diseases by remedies which in the first place stimulate similar conditions, yet we must confess that the contradiction loses its force when everything is considered more carefully than the antagonists of homoeopathy have done hitherto.'

One total cynic remarked that patients treated allopathically died of the treatment, whilst those treated homoeopathically died of the disease. Curiously, for the first time in his life, Hahnemann remained silent to these criticisms. But the next move, this time by the apothecaries, could not be ignored.

On 16 December 1819, the Leipzig apothecaries lodged a 'Complaint to the Council of the Town of Leipzig', in which Hahnemann was accused of infringing their rights and privileges by preparing and dispensing his own medicines. They also reserved the right to name other doctors and students who they complained were also dispensing their own medicines. He was brought before the court on 9 February 1820 when he conducted his own defence and, at the close of the hearing, he stated his intention of handing in a written deposition to precede the final judgement.

The deposition, which ran to more than 5,000 words, was handed in a few days later. Hahnemann's defence was based principally on his assertion that his new system of treatment was

quite different and required only simple medicines, which needed
no compounding, and should therefore be exempted from the
rights reserved for apothecaries. In any case, he reasoned that
since the apothecaries charged according to the weight of the
ingredients in a prescription, the infinitesimally small homoeopathic dose would not earn them anything!

According to the text given by Franz Hartmann (*Allegemeine
Hom. Zeitung*, Vol. 26, 1844), Hahnemann wrote:

Most Humble Representation,

Non debet cui plus licet, quod minus est non licere [That which is
less, may well be allowed to him to whom more is allowed]. My
method of treatment has nothing in common with ordinary
medical science, in fact it is exactly the opposite, and the existing
measurement of medical prescribing can in no way apply. The old
method of treatment requires compound medicines, each consisting of several ingredients of considerable weight. The compounding of these prescriptions requires skilful, often laborious
preparation and takes considerable time, whilst the physician who
is busy with his patients has not always the skill or the time to do it
himself. . . . The dispensing of these complex formulae is the right
of the pharmaceutical chemist, *by the only right, which is exclusively
reserved* for them by Royal Decree.

The new science of treatment—homoeopathy—has no prescriptions to hand over to the chemists and no compound
remedies, but only a single, simple remedy for each single case of
disease. The word 'dispensing' does not, therefore, apply. . . .
Where do we find one single, clear syllable in all the Royal Decrees
which forbids doctors to give simple remedies to their patients? In
my new *Organon of the Art of Healing* (2nd Edition, 1819), on the
science of homoeopathy, my teaching is to use only one simple
substance. . . . The infinitesimal size of the dose of a simple
medicinal substance in homoeopathy, removes all possible
suspicion that the dose may be harmful to the patient. The
apothecaries smile at these small doses and cannot accept their
strong curative power which has been demonstrated, because the
senses as well as *chemical analysis cannot detect any active ingredient*
. . . the homoeopathic physician himself would not be able to
detect the small doses unless they had been dispensed under his
own eyes, and could not find out whether the chemist had
dispensed the right remedy or even put in nothing at all. He can

only rely therefore on his own medicine. . . .

The apothecary earns according to the tariff of the present day, which are all estimated according to the weight of the ingredients in a prescription, and on the labour of mixing them. For a homoeopathic prescription he would earn what amounts to nothing . . . if the apothecaries of Leipzig still insist on their illegal demand they would therefore earn nothing and be obliged to force themselves upon homoeopathic physicians as assistants. . . .

Curiously, he ended his defence by disassociating himself from his pupils: 'Finally, so far as my pupils are concerned, I am not in any way connected with them and I do not represent them. . . . Dr Samuel Hahnemann, Leipzig, 14 February 1820.'

A month later, the Leipzig Court gave judgement against Hahnemann, forbidding him to prepare or dispense his medicines himself for anyone 'under a penalty of 20 talers, and to give no cause for more severe regulations'. The Court stated that the judgement would be valid after confirmation by the State Authorities and the date was duly set as 30 November the same year.

It was nearly four years since the cousin of the King of Saxony, Prince Karl of Schwarzenburg, as Commander in Chief of the Allied Armies, had led his victorious troops through the gates of Leipzig. Prince Karl was a brilliant strategist and a disciplined soldier who had become a national hero in his native Austria and famed throughout Europe. When not on active service he lived on his vast country estate with his wife, the Countess Nani of Hohenfield, whom he adored. On 13 January 1817, the Prince, who had been a heavy drinker, suffered a stroke which paralysed his right side and led to acute insomnia. When their treatment did not improve his condition, his doctors, the Royal physician, Dr von Sax and his Army physician, Dr Marenzeller, recommended that he should be treated by the celebrated Dr Samuel Hahnemann of Leipzig. Hahnemann replied to this request that he would be honoured to treat the Prince, but under no circumstances could he travel to the Prince's home in Austria as, apart from his age, he could not leave his practice or research for a long time.

Ironically, only a year earlier, the medical advisor to Emperor

Franz I had persuaded him to issue a decree forbidding the practice of homoeopathy in Austria, so Hahnemann could not have treated the Prince in his own country in any case! Hahnemann's contemporaries were astounded that he should decline an offer from such a powerful and influential person as Prince Karl, but by then Hahnemann's reputation was so great that the Prince readily agreed to get up from his sick bed and make the journey to Leipzig. He arrived with his two physicians and a large retinue of servants late in April, 1820, and took up residence on the outskirts of the city on an estate called 'Milchinsel'.

Johann Goethe, now world famous himself, was treated homoeopathically, and became so impressed that he referred to Hahnemann in his writings on several occasions. On 2 September 1820, he wrote from Jena:

> Dr Hahnemann is now certainly a world famous physician. This man's doctrine is that the millionth part of any given potent drug will restore any man to the most perfect health . . . I now believe more than ever in this wonderful doctor's theory as I have experienced its efficacy. . . . If it should benefit the Prince of Schwarzenburg, just now staying in Leipzig for this very cure, as much as me, the doctor's fame and reward will not suffer.

It did benefit the Prince, and he responded well to Hahnemann's homoeopathic treatment. He wrote to his wife, the Countess Nani, and to friends in Austria informing them that his attacks had been alleviated and his condition was improving. Hahnemann's precarious legal position, however, prompted the Prince to take up the case on his behalf and use his influence in high places. Haehl (1922) recorded that his action was motivated by his gratitude for services rendered to him, but although this was probably true, the Prince was also anxious to ensure that his treatment would continue, as confirmation of the judgement of the court was imminent.

To the King Friedrich of Saxony, whom it will be recalled, had been his captive at the Battle of Leipzig, he wrote:

Leipzig, 8 July 1820

Your Majesty,
    The rumour is spreading here that Dr Hahnemann, whose treat-

ment I am undergoing at present, will be refused by a decree of the Government the right of treating patients in accordance with his new system. Therefore, I respectfully take the liberty to humbly request Your Majesty to grant an audience to my Adjutant General, Colonel Baron Wernhardt, to allow him to put before you a few disclosures on the method of treatment of Hahnemann which I was able to acquire while under the care of this physician.

Your Majesty's Most Humble Servant,
Karl, Prince of Schwarzenburg.

The King replied as follows:

Castle Pilnitz, 14 July 1820

To My Cousin, Noble Prince, especially dear friend,

The Colonel Baron Wernhardt, whom you have sent, has already delivered your message in connection with the matter of Dr Hahnemann of Leipzig. . . . I have ordered all that is necessary to be done and at the same time that no further steps shall be taken against him. In any case, he shall not be hindered in his efforts to cure you, dear friend, with his new method of treatment.

Your affectionate friend,
Friedrich, King of Saxony.

This letter was enclosed with a letter from a secretary of the King, which read:

The enquiries made by His Majesty's order showed that it is not a matter of forbidding Dr Hahnemann to practise his new method of treatment but owing to the apothecaries of Leipzig laying a complaint before the City Council, the latter are on the point of forbidding Dr Hahnemann from dispensing his own medicines. . . . Congratulations on the restoration of your health.

But the improvement in the Prince's health was short-lived. Haehl reported that not only did the Prince fall back into his old drinking habits, but his personal physician, Dr von Sax, interfered with his own treatment in opposition to Hahnemann's homoeopathic treatment. It was also mentioned that, on what proved to be Hahnemann's last visit, he found other doctors carrying out a venesection on the patient. As the Prince's carriage took him back to Burgstrasse, Hahnemann must have realized that, having lost the co-operation of his patient and with the interference of other doctors, the Prince's position was hopeless. Prince Karl died from another stroke on 15 October 1820, five weeks later. Hahnemann had not visited him again and had probably given up the case.

Four days later, exactly seven years to the day after his triumphant ride through the streets of Leipzig, the Prince's body was drawn on a hearse with all due pomp and ceremony through the same streets. Hahnemann, his lips sealed and his conscience clear, walked behind the hearse with the other mourners to the city cemetery. Hartmann (1844) recorded: 'He was so consciously proud of the knowledge that he had done his duty, that to show his respect for his patient, as well as to show how little he cared for the ridicule of the people, he accompanied the remains of the Prince to Leipzig on foot.'

The post mortem report on the Prince of Schwarzenburg's body showed that the size of his heart was twice its normal size and the walls of the right ventricle were extraordinarily thin; it concluded that he died from a stroke and that his condition was incurable under the circumstances. It was signed by Hahnemann, Professor Clarus, Dr von Sax and a Dr August Bock. The document might have been accepted without further comment but Professor Clarus, Head of Clinical Science, and Hahnemann's old adversary at Leipzig University, decided to add a postscript in which he took a malevolent swipe at Hahnemann's homoeopathic treatment. He opened with the hypocritical comment that he did not envy Hahnemann in the least the fame he had acquired in the treatment of the Prince. He went on to state that homoeopathy was harmful in that it delayed the application of 'strong measures'. The 'strong measures' to which Clarus had alluded would, of course, have included copious blood-letting, stomach rending emetics, violent laxatives and purgation.

The death of the Prince of Schwarzenburg, not only cleared the way for Hahnemann's persecutors to press for a court decision on the matter of dispensing his own medicines, but gave them further ammunition to use against his new therapy. Under pressure from the apothecaries, the Government brought forward their decision on the findings of the High Court from the original date of 30 November. With King Friedrich now less inclined, under the circumstances, to give Hahnemann the protection he had promised the previous July, the court ruling proved to be a poor compromise. It stated that Hahnemann would be allowed to dispense his own medicines, only,

1. When in the country, where their procuration might be made difficult by the distance from the nearest town.
2. In serious cases when the imminent danger does not permit the medicines prescribed to be obtained from the apothecary.
3. In outlying districts where there are no apothecaries.
4. In providing medicines to the poor, when the cost may not be taken from the poor-box or other source.

These concessions were virtually the same as those given to every doctor at that time and, in Hahnemann's case, restricted his homoeopathic practice to the point where for all practical purposes it was impossible for him to continue.

During the next few months, Hahnemann endured the most bitter, sustained and acrimonious attacks he had ever experienced in his long stormy career. Now, his University colleagues, goaded by Professor Clarus, were ostracizing him, and the persecution included his pupils. In his *Origins and Fight for Homoeopathy*, Ameke (1884) mentioned the case of Dr Karl Franz, who, when a female patient of his died of tuberculosis, was charged by none other than Professor Clarus as being responsible for her death for employing homoeopathic treatment. The unfortunate Dr Franz was forced to retire and pay costs, although the charges were not substantiated.

Dr Christian Gottlieb Hornburg, who like Karl Franz, was one of Hahnemann's original team of provers of the homoeopathic medicines, suffered even worse persecution. A brilliant, cheerful youth, he entered the University of Leipzig in 1813, at the age of twenty to study theology. He soon became one of Hahnemann's firm disciples, but eventually he suffered a martyr's fate. His self-assured manner and his support for Hahnemann brought him into conflict with Professor Clarus and his tutors, who twice failed him in his final examinations.

Hartmann recorded that, in 1821, by the instigation of Professor Clarus, both Franz's and Hornburg's homoeopathic medicines were confiscated from their homes by order of the High

Court of the University. In a bizarre ceremony, the medicines were carried away by an Actuary and two beadles and buried symbolically in the church yard of St Paul's, Leipzig. Hornburg appeared before the courts of justice on several occasions in the years that followed, culminating in 1831 in criminal proceedings instituted by the implacable Professor Clarus, following the death of one of Hornburg's patients. After a series of interrogations over a period of two years, Hornburg was pronounced guilty of 'illegal healing and prevention of proper treatment' and sentenced to two months imprisonment. He died of a haemorrhage three days after the verdict on 28 January 1834.

Returning to the winter of 1820-21, whatever his followers and pupils were suffering, Hahnemann himself was still bearing the brunt of the vicious campaign of persecution and events were rapidly moving to a climax. On 5 February, the *Leipziger Zeitung* published a long article in the name of thirteen Leipzig doctors—inevitably including Dr Clarus—which was directed against Hahnemann. This attack resulted from an article Hahnemann had written a few months earlier in another Leipzig newspaper, the *Leipziger Tageblatt*. In this article Hahnemann had declared that the eruptive fever which was prevalent in the city at that time was not scarlet fever, for which *Belladonna* would have been an effective treatment, but 'purpura miliaris'. His motive for writing this article was to inform his fellow doctors that *Aconite*, and not *Belladonna*, should be used to treat this epidemic. He mentioned that he had recommended this remedy in his *Organon of Rational Medicine*, but it was not being used as the doctors had not bothered to read it. He concluded with the words, 'I write this for the benefit of the people of Leipzig, to whom I feel at least bound to show my deep veneration, as it has now become impossible to serve them actively.'

The article, written by the thirteen doctors, refuted Hahnemann's statements and recommended that *Belladonna* was to be prescribed for scarlet fever. They went on to state that Hahnemann did not discover *Belladonna* as it was known before his time.

The following day, on 6 February, one of Hahnemann's colleagues, Dr Moritz Müller, had a letter published in the same newspaper in which he supported Hahnemann, confirming the efficacy of *Aconite*, 'first recommended by Dr Hahnemann.' But a few days later Hahnemann wrote his own reply in his usual spirited style, although by this time, as his earlier article in the *Leipziger Tageblatt* had suggested, he was thinking of giving up the unequal struggle, and leaving Leipzig. 'Just look now', he remonstrated, 'There stand thirteen gentlemen—colleagues of mine in this town—who are struggling hard to show the readers that they envy my reputation (such as it is), my discoveries, my writings (which they will not read) and my cures, which by the grace of God I have successfully effected on patients.' He went on to prove that *Belladonna*, as a cure for scarlet fever, and *Aconite* as a treatment for purple fever, were his own discoveries.

Meanwhile the Leipzig apothecaries had made a further attempt to restrict the limited privileges allowed by the High Court decision even further and have Hahnemann forcibly removed from the city. Their new complaint to the authorities expressed their fear that Hahnemann would abuse these privileges. On 21 February their representation was rejected in a statement 'that matters must remain as determined by the Royal judgement'. The statement added, however, that they should report individual cases of misuse occurring from this cause.

The final move in the battle was again in Hahnemann's favour. It was initiated by the Town Clerk of Leipzig, Dr Volkmann, who entered a protest at the treatment of Hahnemann by the doctors and apothecaries at the Appeal Court of Dresden. The appeal was also signed by a Dr Lindner and forty Leipzig residents. The Appeal Court upheld the protest and ruled that Hahnemann would be allowed to remain in Leipzig. But it proved to be only a rearguard action, for Hahnemann had already decided to leave Leipzig. Having closed his practice and resigned his position at the University, he left the city for Köthen in June 1821. Hahnemann had lost this battle, but not the war.

7.
LIFE IN KÖTHEN
(1821-1835)

Only freedom from prejudice and tireless zeal avail for the most
holy of the endeavours of mankind, the practice of the true art
of healing.

From this time forward, Samuel Hahnemann decided to adopt a
low profile. The years of bitter strife and recriminations had taken
their toll; he had wisely decided to go into semi-retirement and
stay aloof from any further conflict. His thoughts were well
expressed in a letter he had written to a friend:

> In regard to vexations about insults, he who does not remain
> master of himself, does not treat them with indifference, but
> allows his mind to be embittered, poisoned by them, will not live
> long. What an odious thing it is to be overcome by anger! Try to
> keep from you all sensitiveness in regard to such things that
> nothing can deprive you of your composure, your God-given tran-
> quillity. Take warning, learn this beautiful lesson.

Clearly, he had learned the lesson himself, although there were
some notable lapses on his part in the years which followed.

It is often asked why homoeopathy was opposed so strongly as a
new system of medicine. It is difficult to understand why an
intrinsically safe and humane new therapy should have evoked
such a vicious, vehement and sometimes hysterical opposition on
the part of the allopathic doctors and apothecaries. By its very
nature, homoeopathy might have been expected to be received
sympathetically, and even its detractors would surely have
presented their criticisms in an unemotional, scientific manner.
After all, although they did not involve fundamental changes,
new medical systems put forward by Brown (1735-1788) and

Broussais (1772-1838), during Hahnemann's lifetime, were generally adopted.

It is easier to understand the reaction of the apothecaries, since they were obviously motivated primarily by mercenary considerations, whereby they saw homoeopathic medicines as a threat to their livelihood. Apart from Hahnemann and his followers bypassing them by preparing their own medicines, their system of charges at that time was based on the quantity of the medicines they provided; thus, as Hahnemann wrote in his deposition to the court, the infinitesimally small homoeopathic doses required would have proved wholly uneconomic. Another influence on the apothecaries was their, often corrupt, relationship with the doctors of the old school of medicine, whereby the price the patients paid for their medicines was decided between them. At this time, the profession still had more than its share of charlatans. In spite of advances in chemistry, the extravagant claims of the tricksters for the transmutation of base metals into gold or the discovery of the 'elixir of life' had not yet passed entirely into history.

The doctors' motives were less obvious and more complex. Hahnemann's iconoclasm enraged the medical establishment, personified by Professor Clarus and those of that ilk. Down the centuries the status quo, in any sphere of activity, naturally excites a fiercer loyalty than the barely known innovation. Medical practice, in particular, in the early nineteenth century had undergone no fundamental change over hundreds of years and was rooted in tradition. The profession was decidedly reactionary and opposed to change. Paracelsus, three hundred years before, had scorned the physicians for rejecting chemical science: 'What light do you shed, you doctors of Vienna and Leipzig? About as much light as a Spanish fly in a dysentery stool!'

Moreover, the system of teaching in the medical schools was aimed at rigid conformity with accepted practice, and any system not included in the undergraduate syllabus was automatically suspect, for no other reason than *because it was not included in the syllabus.* The exclusion of homoeopathy from the syllabuses of the University Schools of Medicine, even today, is an important factor in determining its acceptance in modern medicine— indeed, a 'Catch 22' situation.

Professional jealousy on the part of the less able doctors was another more obvious motivation at a time when a code of ethics governing professional behaviour was virtually non-existent. It is only fair to mention, in this respect, however, that Hahnemann's own dogmatic and inflexible attitude and his sensitivity to criticism did not help matters. As far as he was concerned, it was homoeopathy or nothing at all. Professor Puchelt had some justification for his view that Hahnemann's theory might not have been so contradicted if he had not declared open war on the rest of medicine.

A less obvious factor, however, which contributed to the doctors' rejection of homoeopathy's compassionate philosophy was founded on the doctor-patient relationship as it then existed. The doctors had not yet won the professional status they rightly enjoy today and in general their relationship with patients tended to be based on fear, not without intimidation. Thus, the doctor might take full advantage of the superstition and the fatalistic attitude of his patients, which induced in them a morbid hypochondria.

He could also rely on the general supposition that the efficacy of any treatment was directly proportional to its harshness and the pain and discomfort it caused. It was this philosophy, coupled with the thought that such small doses of medicine could not possibly be effective, which may have prompted an American professor in 1831 to refer scathingly to 'the little fist which homoeopathy shakes at the giant of disease'. Homoeopathy, which offered a safe, gentle, patient-orientated treatment and treated people as people and not as disease bearers, rocked the established pattern of medicine to its foundations and was to be resisted at all costs.

From the theoretical standpoint, Coulter (1973) took Hufeland's (1826) view, when he described it as a conflict between the allopathic analysis of disease in terms of the causes and the homoeopathic analysis in terms of symptoms. In the era before Pasteur, the idea of cure through 'similars' seemed illogical to the orthodox mind. He suggested that allopathic hostility was rooted in a reluctance to adopt time-consuming homoeopathic procedures and the complications it entailed. Had homoeopathy been a simplified therapeutic doctrine to relieve the doctor's burden, it might have become part of medical orthodoxy.

Returning to Hahnemann's departure from Leipzig. His post-script in his article in the *Leipzig Tageblatt* '. . . it has now become impossible to serve them [the people of Leipzig] actively', intimated that before the end of 1820, he had decided the position was hopeless—at least six months before he left the city. The problem was that he preferred to stay in his native Saxony, but the local authorities would apply the same restrictions on self-dispensing wherever he settled.

Rejecting an offer from Prussia, where the regulations for the dispensing of simple remedies were less stringent, Hahnemann wrote to a freemason friend, Dr Billig in Altenburg in Saxony:

Leipzig, 5 February 1821.

Most Worshipful Ordensbruder
[Worshipful Master of a Masonic Lodge]
Esteemed Friend,
    From the public proceedings directed against me by the Saxon medical men you will have learned how bitterly my method of treatment and myself are persecuted in this country. This persecution has now reached its climax, and I should indeed bear a grudge against the beneficent science and myself if I remained here any longer, and did not seek protection in some foreign country.
    Some propositions of this kind have been made to me from Prussia but I should prefer to spend my few remaining days (I am an old man of sixty-six) in Altenburg. In a country that is so mildly governed as Altenburg, and where I may still meet with true free-masons, I shall be more comfortably settled, especially as twenty-four years ago I enjoyed the great distinction as physician to the dear old Duke Ernst, in Gotha and Georgenthal.

His last statement in this letter was not strictly accurate for, although Duke Ernst of Saxe-Coburg-Gotha was, indeed, his benefactor during his stay in Georgenthal, the physician to the Duke at this time was Dr Buchner. It will be recalled that, much to his regret, Hahnemann had failed to gain the post when the court physician died.

Hahnemann concluded the letter by asking Dr Billig to use his

good offices with the President of the local government to allow
him to settle in a village near Altenburg, where he might practise
homoeopathy unhindered.

When this approach failed, Hahnemann turned to yet another
small, autonomous central German principality, Anhalt-
Köthen, in the person of its ruler, Grand Duke Ferdinand. There
were a number of reasons why he should have made this choice.
First, Duke Ferdinand was his patient; he had been
recommended to the Duke by a former patient he had cured,
Governor von Sternegg, one of the Duke's courtiers. Second,
both these men were freemasons; Hahnemann's correspondence
showed clearly that he was prepared to take every advantage of
the benefits of membership of a lodge as was the custom in those
days. Third, the Duke was a Protestant, although together with
his wife, he was later converted to the Catholic faith. Haehl
(1922) suggested that another reason was that Köthen was close
to Leipzig and the centre of German intellectual life.

Duke Ferdinand of Anhalt-Köthen had distinguished himself
in the capture of Longwy and Verdun and subsequent campaigns
when fighting with the Prussian army against France. He was
finally forced to surrender after the defeat of the Prussian army at
the Battle of Jena in 1806, when he retreated into Bohemia. An
able administrator, he assumed the ducal power over Anhalt-
Köthen in 1818. His wife, Duchess Julie was the daughter of King
Friedrich II of Prussia.

That Duke Ferdinand of Anhalt-Köthen was Hahnemann's
patient emerged from a letter from the Duke, written a month
before Hahnemann left Leipzig:

Köthen, 21 May 1821.

. . . I have been using your medicine all the time, and even if I do
not feel that I have completely recovered, yet it seems to me that
the vertigo has subsided a little.

I have enough medicine to last until the 27th of the month, and
therefore ask what is to happen after this date, if you wish to send
me a fresh supply or not. Moreover, I shall be pleased to see you
here very soon.

Ferdinand, Duke of Anhalt-Köthen

Hahnemann had written to the Duke exactly two months before, requesting his permission to take up residence in Köthen and practise his healing method unrestrained, preparing the remedies 'with my own hands, and be allowed to give them to my patients.'

The Duke replied as follows:

> To Dr Hahnemann
> Burgstrasse 127, Leipzig.
>
> We reply to his request of the 21st of this month [March] that We willingly give him permission to establish himself in our town of residence, Köthen, as a practising physician. Also in consideration of the fact that in Our country all scientific research is given free play, as an exception to the general rule, We wish to grant him the privilege of preparing with his own hands the remedies required for his treatments and to give them to the patients under his care. . . . We conclude with the desire for the happiest results in all the treatments of Dr Hahnemann, so that his widespread reputation may increase, and give Us the opportunity of giving him proofs of Our esteem and goodwill.
>
> Ferdinand, Duke of Anhalt-Köthen

Haehl located the document granting Hahnemann formal permission to settle in Köthen, in the private archives of the Duke of Anhalt in Zerbst, shortly before the First World War:

> We hereby announce to the Commissioners of the State Administration that we have graciously accorded to Dr Hahnemann of Leipzig, upon his humble request, permission to settle here as a practising physician, and to prepare the remedies required for his treatment, and hence the Sections 15, 17 and 18 of the Medical Regulations, 1811, do not apply to him. In other respects Dr Hahnemann is subject to all the rules and regulations of State and police and to all the regulations of our medical direction and our Commissioners of State Administration will arrange all that is necessary.
>
> Köthen, 2 [or 12] April 1821

Pleased as he was with the Duke's reply, Hahnemann was not entirely satisfied that the wording of the document would give him adequate protection, as it did not specifically rule out the possible intervention of the Köthen apothecaries in relation to the preparation of his medicines. Therefore, he contacted the Austrian Consul General in Leipzig, Adam Müller, with whom he was acquainted, and enlisted his help. This move was most astute on Hahnemann's part, as Müller had a considerable influence with Duke Ferdinand. The Duke had broken off diplomatic relations with Prussia and the small neighbouring state of Anhalt-Dessau, over customs and taxation differences and Austria's anti-Prussian policy made Müller a useful ally. With the help of Governor von Sternegg, Müller obtained the Duke's unqualified approval to his proposals, which gave Hahnemann full immunity from any intervention by the Köthen apothecaries. With the Duke's approval, the newspaper, *Korrespondent von und fur Deutchsland* of 19 April carried the following article:

Public Recognition of Hahnemann

The inventor of the homoeopathic system, Dr Samuel Hahnemann, leaves Leipzig in the next few days, and will establish himself as a practising physician in Köthen. His Serene Highness, the Duke of Anhalt-Köthen, has not only allowed him to do this, but also graciously granted him permission to prepare with his own hands the required medicines and dispense them himself to his patients, without the intervention of the apothecaries. The Medical Council of Köthen has given by this act a praiseworthy example of impartiality and of true regard for the progress of science. . . . Dr Hahnemann could hardly be forbidden the right for preparing and dispensing his own medicines in view of the fact that for twenty years the apothecaries of Germany have consulted his *Apothecaries Lexicon* whenever in doubt. . . . A large number of patients whose treatment was interrupted for several months because of the persecution against Dr Hahnemann will now be able to follow their own inclinations unmolested and our free-thinking century is spared the reproach of having suppressed one of the most remarkable discoveries for the welfare of humanity.

This unreserved praise, albeit by an anonymous writer, must surely have heartened the battle-weary doctor.

On receiving confirmation from Duke Ferdinand, Hahnemann immediately began to prepare his departure from Leipzig. On 25 April he travelled alone to Köthen to find a suitable house. At the end of May he closed his medical practice and resigned his post with the University of Leipzig. By this time it took a brave young undergraduate who would risk persecution as a student of homoeopathy, and attendance at his lectures had dwindled to only seven. He obtained a reference from the University, presented to him as a formal certificate, signed by the Academic Registrar, which stated that no complaint had been registered against him or his family before the academic court and that he had been punctual and efficient in carrying out his duties. It was dated 5 June 1821.

A few days later, on the Whitsun holiday, in the early hours of the morning, a veritable convoy of eleven wooden wagons drew up outside *The Golden Flag* in Burgstrasse, where they were loaded with all the Hahnemann family possessions (it will be recalled that one wagon was sufficient when the family left Georgenthal almost exactly twenty-eight years before). Hahnemann recounted later that this move cost him 600 talers (about £240 at present day values). Franz Hartmann reported that a number of Hahnemann's students accompanied them to the city gate, and two young doctors, Dr August Haynel and Dr Theodore Mossdorf, who had become engaged to their youngest daughter, Louise, travelled with them to Köthen.

Köthen was a small town of some 6,000 inhabitants, lying on a plain thirty miles north-west of Leipzig, between two tributaries of the Elbe, the rivers Saale and Mulde. The town gates and the city wall of the old fortified town still stood and in the centre, surrounded by wide, well laid out streets, was the Duke's palace, dating back to the sixteenth century, and the two Protestant churches. For their first few weeks in the town, Hahnemann and his family and companions stayed at the inn, until they moved to the house he had purchased on his earlier visit, at 270 Wallstrasse. The Köthen town archives reveal an entry dated 13 June 1821:

> His Serene Highness the Duke, by means of a rescript of his Ducal Sovereignty, of 4 April this year, has graciously allowed Samuel Hahnemann, Doctor of Medicine, and lately residing in Leipzig, to settle here and he has acquired by purchase the house of Dr Heinrich, in Wallstrasse No. 270 (later No. 47). He has today, in the usual manner, been added to the number of resident citizens.

The house was situated in a corner of Wallstrasse, close by the city wall from which the name of the street was derived. Stephen Hobhouse visited the street in 1931 and described the house as forming one side of an obtuse angle and quite picturesque with a covered wooden balcony running round the angle of the house. It was a two storey house with a steep roof and a stone paved court-yard which opened into a garden about 120 feet long and 24 feet wide. A path which ran the length of the garden was flanked by beech trees.

Assisted by Drs Haynel and Mossdorf, and his daughters, Hahnemann set up his new medical practice in their new home. A very large entrance hall, a common feature of all middle class houses of those days, lit by a large staircase window, was used partly as a waiting room, and to the left was a smaller consulting room. Opposite the consulting room was Hahnemann's study. In the garden, by an ivy-covered arbour, he had a summer house built where he could write and enjoy the atmosphere of the garden which he had always sort during his travels. sought .

Unfortunately, his garden only partly compensated Hahne-mann for the loss of stimulating, intellectual atmosphere of city life in Leipzig. He had, of course, retreated from his beloved Saxony with some reluctance; he would not have chosen the rural seclusion of Köthen had it not been for the kindness of Duke Ferdinand in giving him the freedom to practise. In any case, he was now in his late sixties and he found it difficult to make new friends. He took a long time adapting himself to his new environ-ment. He was inclined to be short-tempered at times with his family and friends and he also developed a persecution complex. It was clearly a case for him not 'looking a gift horse in the mouth!' In October, the same year in which he took up residence, he wrote to Dr Wislicenus in Berlin, 'I cannot live here quietly much longer because of the many chicaneries and I must seek a new place of abode . . .' And nearly ten years later he wrote in the same vein to Dr Aegidi in Dusseldorf, 'Köthen, 18 March 1831. . . . It was merely on the authority of the Sovereign giving me permission to prepare and give my own medicines that I moved from Leipzig . . . and I came to this miserable hole.' Fortunately, although it was against the grain, he did not indulge in any public retort to further criticisms of his homoeopathic treatment.

In spite of his misgivings about provincial Köthen, Hahne-mann's practice soon thrived and, although he probably missed the stimulation of the battles and antagonisms of Leipzig, he welcomed the peace and quiet which gave him the opportunity to develop his new medical treatment and enjoy life with his family. He continued to treat the Duke, and the Duchess also became one of his patients. The Duke wrote to Hahnemann in 1823:

> While expressing to you my thanks for your medical help over the last two years and assuring you of my complete satisfaction, I wish you to accept the enclosed trifle as a slight recompense for your services. May Heaven preserve you in good health for many years for the benefit of suffering humanity.
>
> Duke Ferdinand

Such was the Duke's admiration for Hahnemann, he insisted that a report of his recovery should be published and that Hahnemann should be thanked publicly. The local newspaper report read:

> Our highly venerated Duke, who was suffering from a dangerous nerve affection, is now out of danger, thanks to the efforts of Dr Hahnemann, so famous for his method of treatment. When the inventor of homoeopathy found a friendly reception as well as protection in this country, where the Sovereign supports every effort for the improvement of science, he scarcely foresaw that by his art he would save the life of his illustrious person . . . In perfect harmony they [the Duke and Hahnemann] meet with the con-sciousness of a feeling of mutual gratitude!

In this report, even Hahnemann's old friend in Gotha, publisher Councillor Becker, could not have done better.

Two years later the Duchess wrote to him before leaving for Paris to be received into the Catholic Church:

> It would be impossible, my dearest Hofrath Hahnemann, for me to start on such a long journey without expressing to you my thanks for all the sympathy you have shown me. Rest assured that my heart remembers such debts. . . . Please be so good as to give me a few words regarding the state of health of the Duke, and remember Julie, Duchess of Anhalt-Köthen.

The title *Hofrath*, mentioned in the Duchess's letter, was granted to Hahnemann on his election as a Privy Councillor, less than a year after his arrival in Köthen, when he became officially the Court Physician. Following the announcement of his nomination in the local newspaper the patent was issued:

By the Grace of God, We, Friedrich Ferdinand, Duke of Anhalt, Duke of Saxony, Engern and Westphalia, Earl of Askanien [etc.] We record and acknowledge herewith that we have graciously resolved to nominate Doctor Hahnemann, resident here, as our Hofrath. We nominate and confirm herewith in the full trust that he may appreciate this nomination as a special favour from Us. This patent is drawn up and recorded under Our seal and signed by Our own hand.

Ferdinand, Duke of Anhalt,
given at Köthen, 14 May 1822.

After the turmoil of Leipzig, the years in Köthen passed quietly in a relaxed atmosphere. The weekly mail coach from Leipzig invariably brought one or two people seeking treatment or bearing requests for medicine from friends. After taking a room at one of the inns, they would proceed along the wide, tree-lined Wallstrasse to the great oak door of Hahnemann's house. There they would be greeted by Eleonore, Charlotte or Louise and invited to sit in the hall by the three large windows to the right of the front door, before entering the doctor's consulting room to the left of the front door. Upstairs, Johanna would be engaged, with her other daughters, in household chores in the living room and kitchen.

In his study, hung on the main wall, was Hahnemann's portrait by the German painter, Schoppe, presented to him in 1829, (the first of many he was to sit for during his remaining years) and miniatures of his daughters by the same artist, all painted during their early years in Köthen. By the window stood the old grand piano, brought with them from Leipzig, which their daughters had been taught to play by Johanna. On the mantelpiece over the fireplace were several clocks which Hahnemann wound himself every day.

His daily routine was governed by these clocks. He rose at

6 a.m. in the summer and 7 a.m. in the winter and took a walk in his garden before his breakfast. At 9 a.m. precisely he was at his desk in his study ready to receive patients until 12 noon. After lunch, which was generally roast beef, mutton or game, or regrettably a delicacy much favoured at the time—roast lark. He did not like veal or pork and only cared for a few vegetables, in particular beans, cabbage or spinach. For drink, he preferred strong beef tea or sweet, mild beer, although sometimes he would take a little wine, if he had guests.

After lunch he would sleep for an hour on the sofa and then return to his consulting room until seven in the evening.

His favourite retreat was his garden. Each evening he would walk to and fro for an hour or so in the garden, sometimes meditatively with his long pipe, or sometimes in the company of Charlotte or Louise. In winter, in the dark, he would patrol the garden with a lantern in his hand. In summer, he would sit in his summer house in the ivy-covered arbour. Here he resumed his literary work with his last major book, *Chronic Diseases, Their Peculiar Nature and Their Homoeopathic Treatment*. Sometimes he received visitors in his garden sanctuary. It was a visiting French physician who, on remarking on the smallness of his garden, was rebuffed by Hahnemann's reply, 'You are right—my garden is small—but see how high it is.'

These years were not uneventful, however, and not without further tragedy for the Hahnemann household. The Hahnemann's youngest daughter, Louise—their 'little Louischen'—had married Theodore Mossdorf (Hahnemann's former pupil who had accompanied them from Leipzig) in the Jacobskirche, one of the two Protestant churches in Köthen. Johanna had opposed the marriage for some time, but she had finally relented. Dr Mossdorf was then working as Hahnemann's assistant and living in the family home in Wallstrasse. In 1824 Hahnemann recommended Dr Mossdorf for an official position at the Court of Anhalt-Köthen and for him to be given the same privileges in preparing and administering his medicines as he himself enjoyed. The Duke readily granted Hahnemann's request:

To Our High State Government,

I have decided, so that the lower ranks of my domestics, who have so far received free medical treatment, may be no longer denied the benefits of homoeopathic treatment, to pay to Dr Mossdorf the annual sum of 60 florins from 1 April, whereas he is to bind himself to treat and provide free of charge with medicine, all those domestics who have hitherto received free medicine and who wish to avail themselves of his help and the homoeopathic method of treatment.

Ferdinand.
Köthen, 28 April 1824.

During the next few years, however, relations deteriorated between Louise and Theodore Mossdorf. Johanna had never liked him and later, even Hahnemann found it difficult to work with him. Louise should have heeded her mother's intuition for they were eventually divorced. Theodore moved away from Köthen and Louise returned to her parents' home. A petition written by Hahnemann to the Duke Ferdinand in 1832 shows clearly that the Duke himself was aware of the circumstances, when Hahnemann emphasized that Dr Mossdorf might still have been with him 'if his moral conduct had only been tolerable.'

In addition to his tireless work in his practice, where the waiting room was always full six days a week, year after year, Hahnemann corresponded prodigiously, although he was then in his late sixties. He answered letters from patients all over the world and corresponded regularly with his beloved sister, Charlotta (until she died), with his old friend Councillor Becker in Gotha, and other friends and colleagues including Dr Gustav Gross, Dr Johann Stapf, Dr Karl Franz, Dr Franz Hartmann, Dr Theodore Ruckert, Dr Karl Aegidi, Dr Carl von Bönninghausen, Dr W. E. Wislicenus, Dr Constantine Hering and Ernst Brunnow. After Hahnemann's death, many of the original letters came into the possession of one of his biographers, Dr Dudgeon, but unfortunately they were lost when the ship taking them to Dr Constantine Hering in Philadelphia was wrecked. A large number of Hahnemann's letters were acquired by another biographer, Dr Richard Haehl, in addition to copies of several articles which appeared in various journals during this period.

An article penned by a layman in *Allegemeine Anzeige der Deutschen* (1821) read:

> The author of this article was induced to read Hahnemann's writings as the result of a successful cure, by which he saved, in fourteen days, a dear brother who had looked in vain for help from other doctors for several years. He admits, therefore, that he wishes to testify to the truth of homoeopathy.

It was probably written by Baron Heinrich von Gersdorff, who befriended Hahnemann in 1824 when he brought his children to Köthen for treatment.

This article, which went on to defend Hahnemann from his accusers, prompted a lengthy retort in the same journal from a Dr Stemler, beginning with a quotation from Goethe which suggested that the homoeopathic 'bubble' would soon burst:

> 'The showy lives its little hour. The true
> To after times bears rapture ever anew'

> . . . lately several lay people have adopted a rather insulting attitude towards physicians in general. But the object of the author of the first article would be more suitably attained if Hahnemann or his pupils would write a more comprehensive book than the *Organon of the Art of Healing* or his *Materia Medica Pura.* . . . [homoeopathy] had gained the approval of lay people and physicians who dislike deeper study and prefer the easier rather than the difficult . . . it is not even a new teaching and lacks almost all scientific basis. The assumed successful cures are mostly due to the healing powers of nature.

The author, after comparing Hahnemann with Paracelsus and others, acknowledge reluctantly that he had discovered several good remedies.

Hahnemann resisted the temptation to reply to this attack, but his good friend and colleague, Dr Gustav Gross of Juterbogk, a member of his original team for the proving of *Chamomilla*, *Aconite*, *Belladonna* and twenty-six other medicines, wrote a series of three long articles demolishing Stemler's case so completely that he was never heard of again.

Johann Ernst Stapf became Hahnemann's most intimate friend and they corresponded regularly from 1813 until Hahnemann died. Of Hahnemann's stature, he was a popular, good natured, talented man noted for his modesty. A graduate in medicine of Leipzig University, he was converted to homoeopathy when he read the *Organon of the Art of Healing*. He was particularly interested in the homoeopathic medicines themselves and from the very beginning, Hahnemann recruited him to carry out provings. 'You have the talents for all that I request of you and you will certainly manage it', he wrote in his first letter to Stapf in 1813, 'I can see this already from the symptoms you have sent of *Chamomilla, Rhus toxicodendron, Pulsatilla, Nux Vomica, China* and *Opium* . . . continue to work in this faithful way. What we are doing in this branch is a religious duty for the benefit of mankind.' Stapf eventually took part in the proving of no less than thirty-two medicines.

The risks Hahnemann, Stapf and their forty-seven co-workers took—as Hahnemann had put it, 'for the benefit of mankind'—in observing the symptoms induced in their healthy bodies is exemplified by a list of some of their recorded effects on taking doses of *Aconite* (Monkshood)—vertigo and dizziness; headache; throbbing on left side of forehead; diluted pupil of the eyes; creeping pain on cheeks; vomiting of bile or blood; pressive pain in the stomach; swollen, distended abdomen; flatulent colic; cold sweat in the palms; creeping pain in fingers; palpitation of the heart; fear of impending death.

Hahnemann's regular correspondence with Dr Stapf reveals a close professional relationship; the letters consisted mainly of long, animated discussions of homoeopathic matters and private denunciations of its attackers. Thus, on 1 September 1825, Hahnemann wrote to Dr Stapf:

> . . . it is not worth trying to obtain Sprengler's essay; the ordinary theoretical arguments (against homoeopathy) which have already been refuted a hundred times are crowded onto one sheet. . . . Do not be afraid because so many bullets are fired against us, they miss the mark and are as light as feathers, and if we are honest they cannot harm us. In six months time or a year all this scribble will be quite forgotten.

And four days later he wrote to Stapf again, 'He [Sprengler] deals with the whole of homoeopathy in ten pages . . . how superficial!'

In the same month. Professor Heinroth published a paper entitled *Anti-Organon*, in which he challenged Hahnemann to grant an entirely false premise that the principle of similarity in emetics for an overloaded stomach or copious venesection in headache and palpitation, etc. when nature's help in the form of a bleeding had not occurred. This paper coincided with another publication entitled *Test of the Homoeopathic System*, by a Professor in Darmstadt, in which he criticized the homoeopathic principles and supported venesection, emetics and other purgatives, for no better reason than that this had been the practice for 3,000 years.

Hahnemann quickly dismissed these arguments when he again wrote to Dr Stapf:

23 September 1825.

Dear Friend,

The network of fallacies which is probably to be found in Heinroth's 'Anti-Organon' (for thank God I do not read such rubbish) does very little damage. It cannot easily be disproved because one must first make comprehensible to the reader the nonsense of the writer, and this is not worth the trouble.

Wedekind's book full of rage and malice contains too many violent and exaggerated assertions . . . their snorting and futile gnashing of teeth can be heard far and near; but it is of no avail. . . .

Hahnemann returned to this theme in another letter to Dr Stapf, dated 22 December 1825:

Wedekind's wretched old book was not worth all the trouble he gave himself nor I presume was Wedekind himself worth it . . . I am very indifferent to it all, for it lies in the nature of things and is bound to happen the more homoeopathy advances. How Dr Jenner's vaccination against smallpox has proved itself everywhere, yet in England so many attacks in print were issued against it that at one time I counted twenty—presumably the paper on which they were printed is now used in grocer's shops for wrapping up cheese!

In view of Hahnemann's decision to keep a low profile and not to answer further criticisms publicly, Dr Stapf published the first periodical for homoeopathy in 1822, entitled *Archiv für die*

Homoopathische Heilkunst (Archive for the Homoeopathic Science of Healing) in order to provide a public platform. Dr Stapf was editor until 1826 when he was joined by Dr Gustav Gross. Dr Stapf contributed numerous articles on every facet of homoeopathy and defended his friend, Hahnemann, loyally over the years.

In recent times, Queen Mary, formerly Princess Mary of Teck (1867-1953) and the Consort of King George V, is often credited with introducing homoeopathy into the British Royal Family. Although Queen Mary certainly revived the family interest in homoeopathic treatment, the author's researches have revealed that this honour belongs to Queen Adelaide, formerly Princess Adelaide of Saxe-Coburg-Meiningen, who became the wife of King William IV in 1818. Queen Adelaide probably learned of homoeopathy from her uncle, Duke Ernst of Saxe-Coburg-Gotha, the same Duke Ernst who had brought Hahnemann to Georgenthal in 1792 as physician in charge of the asylum. Until she left for England, Queen Adelaide lived in her father's ducal palace in Meiningen, only twenty miles south-west of Georgenthal, on the other side of the Thuringian mountains. An evangelist and an excellent wife, she suffered from hypochondria and an obsession with the manner of her 'end', which she dreaded would be on the guillotine following a bloody revolution in England. She led an exemplary existence however, and was a keen homoeopath all her life. Her father, the Duke of Saxe-Coburg-Meiningen was also a firm believer in the value of homoeopathy. On his return from the coronation of King William IV and his daughter, the Duke became ill and stayed in Düsseldorf to obtain homoeopathic treatment from Hahnemann's great friend and disciple, Dr Aegidi. This visit was mentioned in a letter Dr Aegidi wrote to Hahnemann dated 1 October 1831.

In 1835, Dr Stapf, who by this time had become a Medical Councillor for Saxony and was much sought after as a homoeopathic physician, was summoned to England by Queen Adelaide. He had been treating her by post for some time, but her condition was now such that she asked him to travel to Windsor Castle from his practice in Naumburg to treat her personally. On his return

6. Queen Adelaide, wife of William IV, the first royal patron of homoeopathy in Great Britain. (Detail from the portrait by Sir William Beechey.)

home, Johann Stapf stayed in Paris with Hahnemann when they discussed the progress of homoeopathy in England. Queen Adelaide died two years later in 1837, aged 71 years, and was buried at Windsor.

Queen Adelaide was an aunt of Prince Albert of Saxe-Coburg-Gotha, the second son of Duke Ernst. Homoeopathic treatment had become a tradition in his family and when the Prince came from Germany to marry Queen Victoria in 1840, he renewed the Royal patronage of homoeopathy. Another homoeopathic influence in the Royal family may have been Queen Victoria's uncle, Prince Leopold of Saxe-Coburg, to whom she turned frequently for advice on political and family matters until his death in 1865. Dr Frederick Quin, who introduced homoeopathy into England, was Physician to Prince Leopold and his household until he became King Leopold I of Belgium.

Royal patronage now spans more than 160 years to include King Edward VIII (1894-1972) who, as Prince Edward, Prince of Wales, invariably carried his homoeopathic medicines in powder doses in his pocket; his brother, King George VI (1895-1952, who named one of his racehorses 'Hypericum'—winner of the 1,000 Guineas Stakes at Newmarket in 1946—after he had been treated successfully with this medicine; H.M. Queen Elizabeth The Queen Mother; and H.M. Queen Elizabeth II. It is interesting to note that homoeopathy has been especially favoured on the distaff side.

Constantine Hering, who like Hahnemann was a native of Saxony, obtained the degree of Doctor of Medicine at the University of Wuerzburg on 23 March 1826. He was to become one of the founders of homoeopathy in America.

Born in Oschatz, Saxony, on 1 January 1800, the son of a church organist, again like Hahnemann he developed an inclination for botany and medicine and, in 1821, he entered the University of Leipzig to read medicine. In his final year he was asked by his tutor, Dr Robbi, to write an article refuting the principles of homoeopathy, but on researching the subject, he became convinced of its value. The troubled young student wrote to Hahnemann for advice and to offer his services as a prover, to which his kind reply was as follows:

> ... As you wish to procure a Doctor's degree in the old system of
> medicine next spring, I beg and counsel you not to allow your
> homoeopathic opinions to be known by the allopathic physicians
> of Leipzig, least of all by that most implacable of allopaths, Clarus,
> if you do not wish to be rejected at your examination. . . . Yet,
> when you have got your degree and have pitched upon the place of
> your future practice, then fear nothing from the obstacles the
> apothecaries profession will be able to put in your way. . . . I have
> confidence in you and am not afraid of being wrong in regarding
> you as one of the few of my followers who will practise the divine
> art among your afflicted fellow men under the eye of God . . . only
> he who is good can be sure of the support of God, without whom
> we can accomplish nothing. . . . Of your offer to make experiments
> with medicines upon yourself, with the help of your sister, I will
> make use of them when you are in a place and a position to practise
> your medicine.

Constantine Hering did not follow Hahnemann's advice and
abandoned the article, thus annoying his tutors and ruining his
prospects of gaining his degree at Leipzig. To the chagrin of his
family and the disgust of Professor Clarus and Doctor Robbi, he
left Leipzig for the University of Wuetzburg, where he obtained
his Doctorate on 22 March 1826. After some months teaching, he
joined a scientific expedition to South America, sponsored by the
Elector (later King) of Saxony, and there he studied and practised
homoeopathic medicine. During his travels he conducted many
provings of new homoeopathic medicines, notably *Lachesis*
(Bushmaster Snake), *Spigelia* (Pinkroot) and *Theridion* (Orange
Spider).

As he entered the University of Leipzig in the year that
Hahnemann left for Köthen, and he departed for South America
shortly after qualifying, Hering had little opportunity to meet
Hahnemann personally. In spite of this, Hering became his close
friend and loyal follower through their correspondence during
the last fifteen years of Hahnemann's life. In 1833, Dr Hering
settled in the United States of America, where he founded, with
the assistance of Drs Detwiler, Ihm, Bute, Freitag and others, the
North American Academy of the Homoeopathic Healing Art in

Allentown, Pennsylvania. He was one of the founders of the American Institute of Homoeopathy, of which he was the first President. In 1836 he founded the Hahnemann Medical College in Philadelphia. He died of angina pectoris, in Philadelphia where he practised, on the 23 July 1880 and was buried in Laurel Hill Cemetery.

Frederick Hervey Foster Quin was yet another disciple of Hahnemann, who holds the distinction of introducing homoeopathy into England in the late 1820s. Born in February 1799, he was probably the illegitimate son of the Duchess of Devonshire. It seems more than coincidence that her maiden name was Hervey, and Frederick Foster was the name of her first husband. Certainly, Quin enjoyed her patronage all his life.

On completing his schooling in Putney in 1815, he spent a short time in France and then entered Edinburgh University to study medicine. Three years later, when still only twenty, he submitted a thesis on arsenic and was awarded the degree of Doctor of Medicine. Shortly afterwards, in 1821, he was appointed physician to Napoleon in exile on St Helena, but he learned that his patient had died before he embarked.

Dr Quin travelled extensively in Europe, staying in Rome with the Duchess of Devonshire until he set up a practice in Naples. After he was treated successfully with homoeopathic medicine when he was seriously ill, he visited Hahnemann in Köthen on 20 July 1826. This meeting was not particularly successful, but several years later, when he was wholly convinced of the value of homoeopathy, he visited Hahnemann again, this time in Paris, and spent a year studying with him. After his first meeting with Hahnemann, he was appointed physician to Queen Victoria's favourite uncle, Prince Leopold of Saxe-Coburg (later King of Belgium) and he travelled in Europe with the Prince's household. In 1831 he visited Czechoslovakia to study the cholera epidemic.

In 1832 Dr Quin set up a practice in London at 19 King Street (and later at 13 Stratford Place) where he built up a considerable reputation as a physician, wit, raconteur and linguist. He wrote extensively: in 1834 he produced a pharmacopoeia, he wrote several papers on cholera and he corresponded regularly with Hahnemann in Paris until Hahnemann's death. He treated many

7. Frederick Hervey Foster Quin, founder of the British Homoeopathic Society and the London Homoeopathic Hospital (painting
by Thomas Unwins, R.A.).

famous people, including Dickens, Landseer and Thackeray.

Dr Quin established the British Homoeopathic Society in 1844 (later the Faculty of Homoeopathy) and, in October 1849, he founded The London Homoeopathic Hospital (later The Royal London) at 32 Golden Square, about twenty-one years after he had introduced homoeopathy into England. He died in November 1878 after being incapacitated with arthritis for the last twelve years of his life.

Hahnemann's last great work, *Chronic Diseases: Their Peculiar Nature and Their Homoeopathic Cure*, was published in Dresden in 1828. This remarkable book eventually ran to five volumes and more,than 1,600 pages. In the first volume Hahnemann recapitulated the principle of homoeopathy, namely that disease is curable by minute doses of compounds which produce effects on the body similar to the symptoms caused by the disease. He also expanded the homoeopathic philosophy and the administration of the remedies and the increasing effect of higher potencies. He attacked his contemporaries for their methods of treatment of chronic diseases, which, he claimed only served to increase the distress:

> This treatment consisted of a whole multitude of nauseous mixtures compounded by the pharmacists from violently acting medicines in large doses, the separate effects of which they are ignorant, together with the use of the salivating [producing excessive saliva] remedies, the painkilling narcotics, the fomentations, fumigations, the blistering plasters, the exuteries and fontanels, but especially the laxatives, leeches, cuppings and starving treatments. By these means, the vital force was more and more diminished.

He went on to expand on the homoeopathic treatment of the whole person:

> The physician's first duty is to enquire into the whole condition of the patient; the cause of the disease, his (or her) mode of life, the nature of his mind; the tone or character of his sentiments, his physical constitution and then especially the symptoms of the disease.

The last section of the book was a detailed homoeopathic

materia medica which included some new remedies, such as *Sepia* (juice from the sac in the abdomen of cuttlefish) and *Silica*. Whereas Hahnemann's *Materia Medica Pura* consisted of provings in the original sense of the word—on healthy persons—those in *Chronic Diseases* were observations of the effects of drugs on patients, and therefore not so reliable (Campbell, 1980).

Unfortunately, *Chronic Diseases* caused a great controversy, this time not only amongst the allopathic doctors, but even amongst the homoeopathic doctors. Hahnemann proposed a theory that most chronic diseases were hereditary from generation to generation. He gave a name to this taint or broader disposition to disease as 'Psora'. His critics interpreted his theory as blaming all those chronic conditions on the skin disease known as scabies, but this was not what Hahnemann had in mind. The fifth and final volume was published in 1839. In view of the controversy, many doctors agreed that it might have been better if this book had not been written, in spite of its contribution to a deeper insight into homoeopathic treatment.

A happy event for Hahnemann took place on 10 August 1829—the celebration of the jubilee of the award of his Doctorate, at Erlangen fifty years before. The festival had been suggested in May the previous year by several of his friends and colleagues, and Dr Stapf, who was a member of the organizing committee, published the details in *The Archive for the Homoeopathic Science of Healing*. At 9 a.m. the joyful gathering of nearly four hundred homoeopaths from all parts of Germany and many countries in Europe assembled in a room which had been specially prepared for the occasion. On a raised table, decorated with flowers and oak leaves, stood a bust of Hahnemann, by Dietrich, which had been specially commissioned by his admirers and friends. On a side table was a large oil painting in a gold frame, painted by the Berlin artist, Schoppe, together with several lithograph copies.

When the guests had assembled, they were joined by Johanna and their daughters and finally the old man, Hahnemann, was led into the room by Dr Stapf. Baron von Gersdorff gave a short address of greeting and congratulation and placed a wreath of laurel leaves on the bust. A Dr Rummel then presented him with a Festival Programme, written by Dr Stapf in Latin and signed by all 400 people attending. Dr Stapf presented his old friend with a red velvet case containing gold and silver medals and a special edition of the *Lesser Writings of Samuel Hahnemann* in which he had written the following:

10 August 1829

May through these pages the spirits of bygone days pass before you once more. At the same time rejoice in what you have accomplished and fought for in the past, full of labours, now crowned with fame and affection.

E. Stapf

Tributes from all over the world were presented. The Duke and Duchess of Anhalt-Köthen sent a gift of a gold snuff box with the initials 'S.H.' in diamonds, together with personal letters.

My Dear Hofrath,

It affords me very great pleasure to be able to congratulate you on your Doctor's Jubilee. You have done such a great and lasting service to mankind by establishing the system of homoeopathy, which is now spreading through the world, that I gladly include myself among the number of these admirers who have assembled this day to bring you the tribute of gratitude. . . . I would like you to accept a small token of a Sovereign's kind feelings, as well as of the high esteem in which I hold your services.

Ferdinand, Duke of Anhalt-Köthen

Very Esteemed Hofrath,

On this your festival day I too will not omit to tender my sincerest congratulations on your Jubilee. In the wide diffusion of homoeopathy you can see the most beautiful fruit of your many endeavours now ripening for the welfare of humanity.

Julie, Duchess of Anhalt-Köthen

Constantine Hering wrote a congratulatory letter from Paramaribo in Surinam:

18 May 1829

Highly Esteemed Hofrath,

I hasten to send you a hurried greeting and thus my voice will not be absent among the many of your pupils and friends, who will all be giving utterance on this great festival of your life. My joyful homage must be heard because I among your pupils was the fortunate one to be chosen to hoist the flag of victory in the far off land of palms. . . . I feel happy to spread and consolidate your teaching out here. . . . With never changing high esteem, yours,

Dr Constantine Hering

Finally, a 'Diploma of Congratulation' from the Faculty of Medicine of the University of Erlangen was presented to him.

In Dr Stapf's account of the proceedings, written in his *Archive of the Homoeopathic Science of Healing* he wrote, 'Deeply touched by this demonstration of friendship, in this festive hour, the great venerable man spoke words of import filled with heartfelt joy and gratitude.'

Afterwards the company assembled in the garden for convivial conversation and a meeting was held in a local hotel to discuss ways in which 1,250 talers raised by his friends and pupils might be spent. It was agreed that it should be invested pending the founding of a Homoeopathic Hospital, and the occasion was also marked with the formation of the Society of Homoeopathic Physicians. After a banquet, which he did not feel well enough to attend, Hahnemann gave an open invitation to all those present to join him at his home at 6 p.m. It was reported that 'they spent the evening with him in learned and friendly conversation.'

A few days later, Hahnemann wrote a letter of thanks to his friend and architect of this Jubilee, Dr Stapf:

I can bear much joy and sorrow, but I was hardly able to stand the surprise of so many and such strong proofs of the kindness and affection of my pupils and friends with which I was overwhelmed on the 10 August. Now that I gradually regain my mental equilibrium and examine each single gift you presented me with such kindness of heart I wonder more and more of the large number of rich and handsome presents given with such kind attention. I have not deserved it. . . . Convey my cordial greetings and appreciation to our friends Rummel, Gross, Franz and Gersdorff. I remain your devoted S. Hahnemann.

Early in March the following year, Hahnemann's wife, Johanna, became ill with bronchial catarrh and a high temperature. During four weeks in bed her condition gradually declined and in the early morning, shortly after midnight, on 31 March 1830, she died in Hahnemann's arms.

Frau Johanna Henriette died in her sixty-seventh year, having been Hahnemann's wife for nearly forty-eight years.

The same morning Duchess Julie wrote a letter of condolence to Hahnemann:

Köthen, 31 March 1830

I have learned with the greatest distress, my dear Hofrath, of the sad blow which has fallen on you last night. This news caused me all the more consternation as I had no idea that the departed was ill. I beg you be assured of my most hearty sympathy.

Julie, Duchess of Anhalt-Köthen

Hahnemann described his own feelings of grief in a letter to Dr Stapf as 'the most extraordinary state in the world'. 'After great suffering and pain', he wrote, 'she finally fell asleep in our arms on 31 March, after midnight, with the most cheerful expression in the world, to wake up in eternity.'

For an elderly man of seventy-five, this stress, coupled with making the funeral arrangements, contacting his married daughters living elsewhere, and coping with the constant demands of patients calling at his home, all proved to be too much. He suffered a relapse of a kind of nervous fever which sapped his strength and confined him to bed. In fact, he had been confined to his bed for several days before Johanna died, but he got up and visited her bedroom several times each day, without telling her that he was ill himself.

Johanna's character traits have been variously, and probably accurately, described as hard-working, industrious, strong-willed, domineering, self-sacrificing, unromantic, practical, harsh, reserved, domesticated and devoted to her family. Whatever her faults, Hahnemann never wrote or uttered a word of criticism of Johanna during or after their life together.

The verse of William Cowper may well have expressed his thoughts.

But well thou play'dst the housewife's part,
And all thy threads with magic art
Have wound themselves about this heart.

Perhaps the last words on Frau Johanna Henriette Hahnemann (née Küchler), may be left to her youngest daughter, Louise, who wrote a fitting obituary in a reproving letter to her father several years later, when he was contemplating marrying again.

> My dearly beloved father, do listen to me. In recalling my blessed mother, her incomparable traits of character and her virtues, my heart breaks! The blessed departed clung to you for nearly forty-eight years with unchanging fidelity, brought up with you ten children, under the most crushing conditions, wandered with you over a great part of the world under the most dreadful persecutions of the enemies of homoeopathy. She always gladly and willingly sacrificed the last penny of her money, as well as her most valuable jewellery, bedding and clothing, to relieve you and the children from want and to drive away hunger and anxiety. She gave you faithful assistance in all kinds of conditions, comforted and helped you to bear suffering and pain. In the most deadly diseases she offered us her unswerving aid and bore the most terrible persecutions with dignity and she ever inspired the children with the greatest esteem due to you. . . . All honour to her! The most fervent affection and reverence to the dear departed!

Johanna left a small legacy to be divided equally between her surviving daughters, but in a sealed document dated 1 February 1831 they each renounced their share.

> We the undersigned children, all of age, declare herewith that we do not demand from our dear father, Hofrath Dr S. Hahnemann of Köthen, even the smallest part of the dowry of our dear mother.
>   Signed: Amalie (age 42); Frederika (age 36); Eleonore (aged 28); Charlotte (age 26); and Louise (age 26).

A few months after the death of Johanna—in August 1830—Duke Ferdinand died after a short illness. He was succeeded by his brother, Heinrich, and the Dowager Duchess Julie moved from the castle to a pretty house near the town gates. The house was situated in a large garden with an ornamental lake on which there were swans, and it became a landmark for coach travellers from Leipzig approaching Köthen.

Dr Griesslich recorded his impressions of Hahnemann following a visit in 1831. At the age of seventy-seven he found him small and sturdy, with sharp, animated features. White locks now covered his temples and his bald crown was covered with a black velvet cap. His eyes flashed with the fire of youth and revealed an enquiring spirit. His conversation was fiery and fluent, often becoming vehement against the enemies and persecutors of homoeopathy. He would only pause to remove his cap and wipe his perspiring brow, relight his long pipe with a taper and take a drink of sweet beer. His general mode of life was, however, abstemious simple and patriarchal.

Hahnemann rarely left his home in the ensuing years, devoting himself to his busy practice and fussed over by his only unmarried daughter, Charlotte, and by Louise, who had returned home after her divorce. When he was not in his consulting room, he would write extensively to his many friends and reply to the numerous letters he now received from all over the world. In winter, he confined himself to his study and in summer he would doze or meditate in his favourite retreat at the end of the garden until late in the afternoon. He kept fit and reasonably cheerful, but in spite of his daughters' attentions he was lonely, and even after all these years in Köthen, he still did not like the town.

8.

LAST DAYS IN PARIS

Non inutilis vixi

At the end of September 1830, Hahnemann wrote to his good friend, Dr Stapf:

> Traditional medicine and surgery is a much too shameful, cruel business. Just read, for example how it teaches how to mistreat cholera and make it fatal by letting 30 ounces of blood, applying quantities of blood leeches and giving large doses of calomel. . . . Is that enough to rouse the anger of homoeopaths?

His words were propitious, for already Asiatic cholera, endemic in India, especially in the delta of the Ganges, was moving with ever increasing speed through Iran, into Russia, and to Hungary and Austria. The disease was generally believed to have been carried into Germany through the Prussian port of Danzig, aboard a Russian ship. By the summer of 1831 cholera had reached epidemic proportions throughout the whole of Western Europe. This disease is characterized by violent diarrhoea, vomiting, cramps and a high death rate. In Danzig, it soon claimed about 500 victims, and twelve days after it appeared in Halle, 105 people were afflicted and 49 died at the outset. In the small town of Raab, in Hungary, out of 1,655 cholera patients, 827 died.

Against this onslaught, as Hahnemann had predicted, conventional treatment of cholera proved virtually ineffective and both the medical profession and the public were thrown into a state of panic. Dr Gross wrote from Juterbogk, 'The allopaths flood us with suggestions and proposals, which I consider hardly worth reading.'

Dr Beumelburg, a Medical Officer of Health, wrote to Hahnemann:

> In the district of Pruss Holland, eight physicians have been appointed to treat cholera, of whom I am one. Everyone of us has had a quantity of remedies sent to us by a travelling apothecary of which I enclose a list as a joke [no less than 39 remedies were listed]. The local physicians know of no definite method which can be employed with certainty against this terrible disease, and the remedies and instructions are so different and contradictory that no one knows which ought to be chosen. . . . Please advise me how to protect myself from infection and suggest a specific homoeopathiç remedy. . . . Even about the cause of the infection the local physicians have as yet no definite opinion. Some say that cholera is spread through the air, others say that it is contagious.

A Dr Kussman recalled, 'Many physicians saw at that time, the reason for the fatal course of cholera in the thickening of the blood on account of the enormous discharge of fluids. My teacher recommended venesection to thin the blood. I followed his advice and the two poor fellows died.'

Meanwhile, as general anxiety spread, towns and village communities were isolating themselves. For example, every village around Vienna threatened to kill anyone who tried to come there from the city. In the city itself, a flourishing trade grew up in copper pendants hung around the neck as a form of protection against the 'evil pest' and the entire military garrison was equipped with them. Insanitary and unhygienic conditions which prevailed at that time ensured that the disease continued to spread unchecked and to take a staggering toll throughout 1831.

Between June and October that year, Hahnemann wrote four essays on cholera and its homoeopathic treatment. These were entitled, 'Cure of Cholera'; 'Letter About the Cure of Cholera'; 'Surest Cure and Eradication of Asiatic Cholera' and 'Appeal to Thinking Philanthropists Respecting the Mode of Propagation of Asiatic Cholera'.

These essays were given to four different publishers in order to gain the widest possible circulation and Hahnemann charged no fees. By the application of his 'Law of Similars' he was able to describe a curative and preventive procedure based on an accurate report of the symptoms in five cases of Asiatic cholera given to him by his great nephew, who was practising in St Petersburg. Hahnemann recommended pure, undiluted spirit of *Camphor* to be used as a prophylactic and as a treatment in the very early stages, followed in the later stages, which he specified, by *Copper*, *Veratrum album*, *Bryonia* and *Rhus toxicodendron*, the last two in alternation. Conscious of the need for proper hygiene, he added:

> In order to make the infection and spreading of cholera impossible, the garments, the linen etc. of all strangers have to be kept in quarantine (whilst their bodies were cleansed with speedy baths and provided with clean clothes) and retained there for two hours at stove heat of 80°[C]—this represents a heat at which all known infectious matters and consequently the living miasmas are annihilated.

He went on by laying special emphasis on the cleanliness, ventilation and disinfection of rooms. In the light of the work of Pasteur and Lister some thirty years later, this advice seems prophetic, but his views on the causes and transmission of cholera were even more ahead of his time. In the last of his four essays on Asiatic cholera he wrote:

> The most stinking infections took place and made astounding progress whenever in the stuffy spaces of ships, filled as they are with musty aqueous vapours, the cholera miasma found an element favourable to its own multiplication and throve to an enormously increased swarm of those *infinitely small, invisible living organisms* which are so murderously hostile to human life and which most probably form the infectious matter of cholera.

It was not until sixty-seven years later that Robert Koch and others demonstrated the existence and the nature of the disease virus, so accurately predicted by Hahnemann.

Homoeopathic treatment of cholera proved remarkably successful. Of the 1,655 cholera patients in Raab, for example, only six of the 154 patients treated homoeopathically died, whilst of the remainder, 821 (almost 50 per cent) treated conventionally, died.

Reports from other parts of Europe showed that, whilst the death rate amongst patients undergoing conventional treatment invariably exceeded 50 per cent, the death rate amongst those undergoing homoeopathic treatment ranged from a highest level of 21.1 per cent to a lowest level in Vienna of only 2.4 per cent. The figure reported from Vienna was of particular significance because, at this time, the practice of homoeopathy was illegal in Austria. It will be recalled that it was this ban which had forced Prince Karl of Schwarzenburg to come to Leipzig for homoeopathic treatment eleven years earlier.

In spite of this success, Hahnemann still met some opposition. When the danger of cholera infection in Köthen had passed, and only then, a butcher named Kaiser, who was a petty official on a local Commission, wrote to Duke Heinrich of Anhalt Köthen requesting that the distribution of Hahnemann's fourth essay on the treatment of cholera be prohibited unless certain passages were deleted. He reasoned that 'a complete prohibition against printing it here might encourage the author even more to have this piece printed elsewhere and then a private distribution here, which could not be completely avoided, may be even more harmful'.

Although Duke Friedrich had acknowledged the privilege granted to Hahnemann to prepare and dispense his own homoeopathic medicines, his support was weaker than his late brother, Duke Ferdinand. He admonished Hahnemann in a letter date 22 October 1831:

> Notwithstanding my acknowledgement and appreciation of your keen endeavour to procure help for your fellow citizens, I must point out to you, how in view of the existing medical administration, your conduct in no way agrees with those laws, wherefore I wish that you should not extend the privileges accorded to you in your medical practice beyond their limits. . . . I also wish that when expounding your method of treating cholera you would avoid declamations against the allopathic physicians.

Hahnemann replied to the Duke, saying how grieved he was that his letter had presupposed that he was guilty of some offence against the medical laws. In his view, the complaint was inaccurate and unjustified. Finally, he requested permission to provide spirits of camphor as a protective and curative medicine against cholera free to anyone who requested it. To avoid the censorship, he promptly arranged to have his essay published in Leipzig.

Predictably, his action enraged Duke Heinrich who, in the following December, issued an edict:

> Hofrath Dr Hahnemann, residing here, intended a short while ago to publish here an essay on cholera which contained very insulting and defamatory remarks on the allopathic physicians . . . I do not wish that, in my country, a book should be openly sold which might give rise to agitations, disputes and discord. The sale of the book in question, *Appeal to Thinking Philanthropists Respecting the Mode of Propagation of Asiatic Cholera*, published in Leipzig, edited by Carl Berger, cannot be allowed.

It is a matter of conjecture whether the Duke would have permitted the essay to be published in Köthen had Hahnemann tactfully confined his words to the homoeopathic treatment of cholera and refrained from castigating the medical profession, however well deserved.

A month before the Duke's edict, Hahnemann had made his final move in the cholera conflict, when he sent an open letter, addressed to the King of Prussia, Friedrich Wilhelm III, to his old friend Councillor Becker in Gotha. In a covering letter he told his friend that 'the time had come to speak out boldly' on behalf of homoeopathy and his treatment of cholera, and he asked him to publish the open letter in the *Allegemeine Anzeiger der Deutschen*. It began:

> Perhaps You of all the German sovereigns will read this loyal newspaper, and in this way learn what no one has yet told you of the possibility of minimizing the number of cholera victims in Your otherwise prosperous country. Do not let them minimize the losses to you . . . a humanitarian Sovereign like You must be deeply grieved about the loss of life of one faithful subject that could be avoided. . . .
>
> You Great Monarch, who find your only happiness in the welfare of Your subjects, have no homoeopathic doctors (true doctors) in your country, which is otherwise favourable to free intellectual activity your medical potentates have suppressed homoeopathy for fear of being overshadowed by it.

Whether the King of Prussia read the open letter or not, Hahnemann's plea was to no avail, for on 31 March 1832, a Royal Decree was issued withdrawing the right of homoeopathic doctors to prepare or dispense their own medicines. It laid down that all doctors must prescribe their medicines from a pharmacy, and if any homoeopathic doctor had any doubts, they were free to supervise the pharmacist to ensure that he employed the necessary care.

Unfortunately, much of the credit for the spectacular success of homoeopathic treatment of cholera during this epidemic was denied, since most of the results in hospitals, which would now be called clinical trials, were deemed unreliable, as they were not under the supervision of the medical establishment of the day. By the autumn of 1832, the cholera epidemic had run its full course and the whole of Europe sighed with relief.

Between late 1831 and late 1832, during the cholera epidemic, Hahnemann's fifth daughter, Frederika, was murdered. After the death of her first husband, Frederika had married Herr Dellbruck, a Clothing Inspector for the Post Office in Stotteritz, a suburb of Leipzig where the Hahnemann family had lived many years before. They had lived in Dresden until Herr Dellbruck died, when she returned to Stotteritz. Shortly after her return she was found brutally murdered in the garden of her home. Her attacker had ransacked the house and stolen money and bonds and securities. During police enquiries in the Hahnemann home, Amalie was able to give the serial numbers of the stolen bonds, which led to the arrest of a man. Apparently this man approached another man in a Dresden street and asked where he could sell bonds and securities. By chance the other man was a plain clothes policeman and he took the enquirer to the police station, where he was found to be in possession of the stolen bonds. He was arrested and charged with Frederika's murder and imprisoned whilst awaiting trial, but before sentence could be passed he committed suicide by hanging himself in his cell.

On 29 July 1832, Dr Gottfried Lehmann, accompanied by his wife and two daughters, visited Köthen to have his wife treated by Hahnemann. He was born in Leitzkau in 1788, and after qualifying in medicine he devoted himself to the practice of homoeopathy. From their first meeting the two men immediately established a rapport, and Hahnemann, now in his old age, and unable to cope with the influx of patients from all over the world, appointed Dr Lehmann as his assistant. It was a fortunate choice, for Dr Lehmann proved to be a good practitioner who was practical and energetic and complemented Hahnemann perfectly. Hahnemann wrote to his friend, Dr Aegidi on 3 March 1833, 'My assistant Dr Lehmann, an extremely zealous and industrious homoeopath works with me in vain. The two of us cannot cope with the crowd of patients and we shall almost succumb in the struggle—just because we are so successful in everything.'

The Leipzig Homoeopathic Hospital opened on 22 January 1833 at No. 1 Glockenstrasse. The house, which was situated in an outer suburb of Leipzig, was purchased for 3,525 talers, (about £1,400 at today's value), from the funds collected at Hahnemann's Doctorate Jubilee in 1829. It was a three-storied building with an adjoining garden. On the ground floor was a dispensary and a library, which included books donated by Hahnemann two years before, and on the first floor twenty beds were provided. The Association of Homoeopathic Physicians and the Leipzig Homoeopathic Association elected Dr Moritz Müller, an honourable man and an able physician and administrator, as Director of the hospital and Drs Hartmann and Hartlaub were appointed as physicians. In spite of opposition from the arch-antagonist of homoeopathy, Dr Clarus, who, as Medical Officer of Health, opposed the establishment of the hospital on the grounds of poor sanitation in the district, the Government gave its permission for the hospital to be opened.

Hahnemann himself had often expressed the establishment of a Homoeopathic Hospital as his dearest wish and rejoiced at the prospect as the crowning of his life's work. He had written to Bönninghausen in the spring of 1831, 'If only we had a homoeopathic hospital, with a teacher attached to it who could instruct students in the practice of homoeopathy. . . . But who knows how wonderful God's ways are for bringing things about.' In view of these favourable portents, it is surprising that the whole venture proved to be a total disaster!

It is even more surprising that it was Hahnemann himself who was largely to blame for the confusion and acrimony, which eventually led to the closure of the hospital. The discord amongst the homoeopathic physicians had its beginnings with the founding of Dr Stapf's *Archive for the Homoeopathic Science of Healing* in 1822. This periodical had given the homoeopathic physicians, who were rapidly increasing in number, an opportunity to air their often divergent opinions and Hahnemann resented any departure from his pure homoeopathic theory. He was particularly incensed by an article by Dr Moritz Müller in which he put forward the view that homoeopathy should not be exclusive and that both systems of medicine might be complementary to one another. Hahnemann, now old and embittered, regarded this view as a compromise, which he had rejected vehemently in all his teaching. The publication of Hahnemann's *Chronic Diseases* in 1828 with, *inter alia*, the 'psora' theory and higher potencies, led to further differences of opinion between the homoeopathic doctors.

Hahnemann also had a strong distrust of Drs Hartmann and Hartlaub and, understandably in view of his past persecution, of the Leipzig doctors in general. The location of the hospital in Leipzig, with all its bitter memories for Hahnemann, not unnaturally aroused his antipathy. He was also suspicious of the hitherto antagonistic Leipzig Council's support for the hospital and the motives of Dr Moritz Müller in securing the position of its Director.

The last straw as far as Hahnemann was concerned was the revelation that Dr Müller had treated the daughter of a keen supporter of homoeopathy with blood leeches. He promptly wrote to Dr Hartlaub withdrawing his authority to sign the diplomas of the Association of Homoeopathic Physicians, but, more importantly, he wrote a bitter condemnation, clearly aimed at Drs Müller, Hartmann and Hartlaub, in the *Leipzig Tageblatt* of 3 November 1832:

> A Word To The Half-Homoeopaths of Leipzig
>
> I have heard for a long time with displeasure that some in Leipzig who pretend to be homoeopaths allow their patients to choose whether they shall have homoeopathic or allopathic treatment.

Whether they are not yet grounded in the true spirit of homoeopathy or that they are lacking in true love for their fellow mortals
or they have no scruples in dishonouring their profession for the
sake of sordid gain, let them not require of me that I should
recognize them as my true disciples.

It is remarkable that in no place are there such homoeopathic
allopathic mongrels to be found as in Leipzig, a town hitherto so
dear to me.

Blood-letting, the application of leeches and Spanish flies, the
use of fontanels and setons, mustard plasters and medicated bags,
embrocations with salves and aromatic spirits, emetics,
purgatives, etc. are some of the quackeries by which, when used in
conjunction with homoeopathic prescriptions, we are able to
recognize the crypto-homoeopath, trying to make himself
popular. . . . Either be honorable allopaths of the old fraternity or
pure homoeopaths. . . . But he who from this day forward hesitates
to follow this advice, to prove himself in word and deed a
homoeopath, let him never again come to Köthen while I behold
the light of day, for he may look for no friendly reception. . . .

Now, when a hospital is about to be founded for a practical
demonstration of only genuine, purely homoeopathic treatment
. . . I consider it my duty to raise my voice lest these scandalous
abuses should impart in this prospective hospital a disreputable
character to the whole system. Hence I most solemnly protest
against the employment of such a bastard homoeopath, whether
as teacher or medical attendant.

In the shadow of this shattering public reprimand from the
founder of homoeopathy, the opening ceremony of the Leipzig
Hospital was conducted in a subdued and troubled atmosphere.
In the months which followed, attacks and counter-attacks
appeared in the press and homoeopathic journals, accusing and
abusive letters were exchanged and, unfairly, the hospital bore
the brunt of the criticism. Inevitably, the reputation of the
hospital declined, and on 10 April (Hahnemann's birthday) 1832
Dr Moritz Müller, who had earned the highest respect of those
who worked with him, resigned as Director. Six months later he
was succeeded by Dr George Schweikert, a graduate of the
University of Jena and a friend of Professor Hufeland, who had
announced his conversion to homoeopathy in Dr Stapf's *Archive*
periodical in 1825.

Hahnemann was pleased with Dr Schweikert's appointment and he attempted to make amends for his earlier indiscretion. He agreed to visit the hospital and, in June 1834, accompanied by his daughters and his assistant, Dr Lehmann, he arrived in Leipzig for the fifth and last time. A small celebration was hastily arranged and in the evening Hahnemann declared himself thoroughly satisfied with the hospital and agreed to undertake its management himself. As a result, the Board of Directors of the Central Association, who had previously managed the hospital, was disbanded.

Not only did his autocratic action cause further disunity amongst the homoeopathic physicians in Leipzig, but the administration of the hospital from Köthen by an ageing man proved impractical. The hospital fell into financial difficulties and, after two years, Dr Schweikert suddenly resigned his post in favour of a Dr Fickel. This new Director brought further calamity to the hospital and, on his resignation, he even admitted that he had only infiltrated the ranks of the homoeopaths to discredit them. After two more Directors had resigned and a worsening financial position had reduced the hospital to an out-patients department, it was finally dissolved in October 1842.

Mademoiselle Marie Melanie d'Hervilly arrived in Köthen, from Paris, on 8 October 1834. Ostensibly she had come to consult Hahnemann about her health. She was French, having been born and bred in Paris, about thirty years old, intelligent, impulsive, charming and very attractive, with fair hair and blue eyes. In the opinion of many of Hahnemann's professional colleagues and especially his own daughters, however, she was self-indulgent, vain, calculating and shrewd.

Melanie caused shock and consternation among Hahnemann's friends and family from the moment she arrived in Köthen as she was dressed in what was described by a neighbour as 'man's attire'. Nowadays, jeans and chic outfits from fashionable boutiques in London, Paris or New York pass without comment, but in nineteenth century Germany, before the emancipation of women, Melanie was scandalized and contemporary accounts were full of innuendo. Even on her death, forty-four years later, the Anglo-American Journal of Homoeopathic Medicine felt it necessary to publish the explanation that she wore men's clothes 'to protect herself whilst travelling alone from the not unusual insults to womanly modesty', and she showed, therefore, foresight and discretion.

Moreover, Melanie's obvious attentions to their aged father whom they had cared for assiduously since their mother's death, incurred the instant dislike of Charlotte and Louise. Over the next three months, as Hahnemann's relationship with Melanie grew stronger, Charlotte and Louise's dislike of her turned to bitterness, recrimination and even hatred.

Details of Melanie's background were revealed in autobiographical notes, written thirteen years later in 1846, in defence of her right to practice homoeopathic medicine. Born in a large house in Paris between 1800 and 1805 (she never admitted her true age), her father's name was d'Hervilly. During her happy childhood, she studied art and painting and, in her own words, became a very good musician, under the tuition of her father. She had no interest in knitting or other domestic occupations. According to Melanie, her mother, who had married young, became jealous of her as she developed into a young woman. As a result, her father put her in the care of a Monsieur and Madame le Thiere who adopted her as their daughter. She became a successful artist and sold many of her paintings to influential people, including M. Louis Gohier, whom she described as 'the last President of the French Republic' (he was briefly President of the Executive Directory of the French Republic in 1799). It was he who left his name to her in his will, so she became Marie Melanie d'Hervilly-Gohier. She certainly enjoyed social life in high circles and admitted an affinity with older men, particularly those with power and influence.

Melanie held strong views on the barriers men put in the way of women in the intellectual field, preventing them entering the professions, to become musicians, poets, writers, mathematicians or scientists. She claimed she was born with a vocation for medicine having dissected birds at the age of eight, and to have studied anatomy, physiology and pathology in her late teens. Like Hahnemann, she recognized the inadequacy of contemporary medicines. Certainly she proved later that she did have a distinct flair for practising medicine.

Explaining her reason for visiting Köthen, she wrote:

> My health was impaired as a result of grief caused by the loss of several friends. Looking everywhere for help I could not find any, until Hahnemann's *Organon of the Healing Art* fell into my hands and suddenly opened my eyes; at first glance it showed me the whole truth about medicine. On the very same day I resolved to go and visit Hahnemann. I told my friends who considered me mad. I arrived in Köthen on 8 October 1834.

Without warning, Melanie d'Hervilly and Samuel Hahnemann, almost eighty years old, were married in the front room of his house in Köthen, on 18 January 1835. Hahnemann never revealed the events which led to their decision to marry, but Melanie explained that he wished to marry her, and his friends did all they could to persuade her to accept his offer. Haehl (1922) remarked tartly, 'It was not Hahnemann who married her, but she who married him, the young woman marrying the old man. This is, in short, a confession of a clever woman's skilful calculation and of the goal she had set, namely the possession of a man.' No doubt Hahnemann was flattered by the advances of a young attractive woman and, in any case, he had felt lonely since he lost Johanna.

Melanie had overcome all the obstacles to the marriage in a very short time, not least the problem that he was German and a Protestant and she was French and a Catholic. Moreover, Charlotte and Louise were distraught with the announcement of their father's impending marriage. Certainly they could not live in the same house with their stepmother and with Melanie's help, Hahnemann bought a nearby house for them. The marriage took place, therefore, amidst tears and entreaties from his highly strung daughters. The letter, quoted in the previous chapter, written by Louise concerning her mother's virtues, was her final attempt to shame her father into abandoning his plan to marry again.

Letters of congratulations poured into No. 47 Wallstrasse including one from Princess Louise, daughter of King Friedrich of

8. Melanie, Samuel Hahnemann's second wife.

Prussia. She wrote, '. . . My surprise was not small when I read in the local newspaper the announcement of your marriage as I had no idea of it, and I send you all good wishes for your welfare. . . .'

Regrettably, some newspapers carried scurrilous reports which attempted to ridicule the marriage and homoeopathy. For example, the *Dorfgzeitung von Saxe-Meinigen* reported:

> The renowned father of homoeopathy, Dr Hahnemann was married again on 18 January in his eightieth year, to prove to the world how his system has been glorified in him. The young man is still vigorous and strong, and challenges allopathic doctors— imitate me if you can!

The *Allegemeine Anzeiger der Deutschen* leapt to Hahnemann's defence and rightly declared that these reports were wholly lies and infamous slander, and referred to the publisher of the article mentioned above as an arrogant shameless, evil and malicious jester.

On this occasion, Hahnemann was immune to the opinions of others. In a letter to Bönninghausen, the following May, he referred to his heavenly life with his wife, her perfection and described her as an 'angelic wife'. She had also painted his portrait which pleased him.

Although Hahnemann had originally declared his intention to remain in Köthen, he wrote again to Bönninghausen a month later informing him that he was going to accompany his wife to Paris, to arrange her money matters and have a good rest. In the early morning of 7 June 1835, he set out with Melanie on the fourteen-day coach journey to Paris, never to return to Köthen.

Charlotte and Louise followed Melanie and their father in a second coach as far as Halle and, after dinner together at the Kronprinz Hotel, they returned to their home in Köthen. For the rest of their lives they lived as recluses, keeping a candle burning in the hall at night and rarely leaving the house. They shunned visitors, but many years later, in 1872, Dr Constantine Hering was admitted by Louise. Charlotte had died there ten years before. Louise gave him some *Aconite* from a vial used by her father, and she spoke bitterly of Melanie Hahnemann, whom she claimed had lured him from their home and separated him from his family ties to be exploited in a lucrative practice in Paris.

On their arrival in Paris in June, Hahnemann and Melanie moved into a small apartment in the centre of the old city at No. 26 Rue des Saints Peres. The fact that Melanie had reserved this apartment before she left for Köthen is proof enough that she had every intention to return. Finding the atmosphere oppressive in a small apartment in an exceptional heatwave in the city that summer, the couple moved out after only a few months to better and more spacious accommodation at No. 7 Rue de Madame, near the Parc du Luxembourg.

On his eightieth birthday, 10 April 1835, Hahnemann was elected an Honorary Member of the North American Academy of Homoeopathy at Allentown, Pennsylvania. Only two months before he had written to the Gallic Homoeopathic Society in Paris to thank them for their award of an honorary diploma although he had received the award nine months earlier. His belated acknowledgement was no doubt instigated by Melanie in order to prepare the ground for their return to France.

In the same year, Dr August Haynel, who, as Hahnemann's pupil, had accompanied him when he left Leipzig, emigrated to America. After leaving Köthen, he practised in Berlin during the cholera epidemic and then in Merseburg. In America he lived in Philadelphia, New York and Baltimore until he returned to Germany a few years before his death in Dresden in 1877.

The article in *Allegemeine Anzeige der Deutschen*, defending Hahnemann's marriage, had publicly stated that Melanie would receive nothing whatsoever of his property either during his life-time or at his death, and he would immediately assign his property to his children and grandchildren. Accordingly, on 2 June, Hahnemann's will was signed and executed. It stipulated that *his wife was to have free choice of his funeral arrangements* and none of his family were to interfere. It went on to confirm the public announcement made three months earlier, except that all the possessions he was to take with him to Paris would become Melanie's property on his death. It also made another of his intentions clear, quoting Hahnemann thus, 'I am now in my eighty-first year, and naturally desire to rest and to give up all my medical practice.'

A few months after Hahnemann's arrival in Paris, however, no doubt under the influence of Melanie, his intentions were reversed. Not only had he signed a new will leaving all of his property to his wife, but he had set up a medical practice! Apart from Hahnemann's own comment in his will, Melanie had often stated, before and after their marriage, that her wish for him was 'a quiet, peaceful rest from his labours'. The first German newspaper to publish the notice read, 'By a Royal Decree (King Louis Philippe) of 12 August, Dr Hahnemann, who has already been staying in Paris for some months, has been granted the right to practise'.

Under the influence of Melanie, permission had actually been granted by the Minister of Public Health at that time, a Mr Guizot, in spite of the refusal of the Medical Faculty of Paris. The date of Hahnemann's original appeication to Mr Guizot was most significant—13 February—whilst he was still living in Köthen.

The arrival of Hahnemann, the founder of homoeopathy, in their midst, was greeted with great rejoicing by the homoeopathic doctors in France, The Gallic Homoeopathic Society had been formed in 1832 and they had already awarded him their honorary diploma. It was in an atmosphere of great excitement, therefore, that Hahnemann appeared at a festival organized by the Society to celebrate his taking up residence in France. After a brief speech of welcome, he was conducted ceremoniously to a seat of honour by the Society's President, Dr Leon Simon, who then read a speech prepared by Hahnemann:

> I have come to Paris for the furthering of homoeopathy and am most happy to be amongst you. I thank the French Government for the freedom which it grants to our Society and our activities. . . . My long and successful practice proves that pure homoeopathy, practised by those who have thoroughly studied and completely grasped it, is in itself sufficient for all the needs of suffering mankind.
>
> I thank the French Society for their works. I am pleased to see among them industrious and keen young men who will continue that which they have so happily initiated. I am deeply touched by the expressions of affection which I have received from all its members. I combine my zeal with theirs, and will support their endeavours for the furtherance of our divine science, because old

age, which has never diminished its march, has not chilled my
heart nor weakened my thoughts and homoeopathy will always
remain the object of my heart. . . . When we are dealing with a
science which is concerned with the saving of life, *it is a crime to
neglect its study.* . . . I am confident that you will succeed as I hope
that you will always remain united in heart and principle.

At the close of the festival, Hahnemann was elected Honorary
President for life. He often attended subsequent meetings when
he occupied a special seat of honour which was kept vacant when
he was absent.

Not only did Melanie promote his practice, but she began to
participate actively by treating a number of patients herself,
although she was medically unqualified. This fact emerged in a
letter from Hahnemann written to a Dr Hennike in Gotha on 16
December 1837:

Rue de Milan, No. 1, Paris

. . . I am feeling much better and happier under the unceasing care
and unprecedented love of my dear Melanie, than I was during the
last years in Köthen. She treats a large number of poor patients
daily, free of charge, under my supervision, which, however, she
hardly needs now, because through her own study of homoeopathy she daily progresses more and more. . . . Every Monday
evening, from eight to half past ten, a number of the best doctors
gather here in my spacious house for discussion on homoeopathic
subjects. . . .

Yours,
Samuel Hahnemann

This letter confirmed that he had moved house once again. His
new home in the Rue de Milan, at the corner with the Rue de
Clichy, was a large mansion built at the end of the eighteenth
century.

Hahnemann's remarkable success with his homoeopathic
treatment, coupled with Melanie's flair, personality and
ambitious drive proved to be an irresistible combination. By the
late 1830's his practice had become the most celebrated in
Europe. Dukes and Princes, prominent politicians and poor
people alike flocked to the Rue de Milan for treatment. He was
inundated with requests from other doctors to be allowed to work

with him as his pupils. Melanie had plucked the old master from his well-earned retirement and set him up again to work harder than he had ever done. Not that he complained. Writing to Bönninghausen in January 1836 he spoke of his happiness and love for Melanie, which he said increased daily. He thought that no husband could be happier on earth, in spite of a 'large amount of work', since his house was never free from friends and people seeking help.

The luxurious opulence he enjoyed a 1 Rue de Milan was in marked contrast with Hahnemann's poverty-stricken days in Stotteritz and even his somewhat frugal and austere existence in Köthen. Contemporary accounts described his house as a palatial building surrounded by a high wall with large iron gates opening into a spacious court. Each workday morning a group of poor people would gather at the gates and a long queue of carriages—hackney and private—some of the latter with coats-of-arms on the side panels, would form along the whole length of the Rue de Milan, spilling out into the Rue d'Amsterdam. The carriages moved forward every few minutes until they finally drove through the gates where the patients alighted at the front door. Here several footmen in full livery received them in a large hall and conducted them up a wide staircase, where more footmen ushered them into an elegant salon.

Most of the rooms were decorated with fine paintings, many painted by Melanie herself, elegant velvet couches, sculptures and costly vases, many of which had been presented to Hahnemann by grateful patients. Some rooms displayed medals, diplomas and awards presented to him by learned societies from Europe, America and South America.

During his patients' long wait, often three hours or more, Melanie would appear and circulate amongst them. Elegantly dressed, with her flaxen hair in a knot at the back of her head and with some ringlets behind her ears, she greeted each person in turn, engaging some in polite conversation and occasionally stooping to kiss a child. Eventually, a valet would appear in the waiting salon and announce that the doctor was ready to receive a particular patient. He would lead them to the door of Hahnemann's consulting room and announce their names in a loud voice. His consulting room was more simply decorated than the other rooms, which from what we know of Hahnemann's character, might have been expected. He would sit in an armchair, dressed in an expensive smoking jacket, with his head covered by a velvet cap around which hung snow white locks of hair. He usually smoked a long pipe reaching down to his knees, which he removed from his mouth as he stood to bow and greet his patients.

Invariably, Melanie would be present during Hahnemann's consultations. She would seat herself at a desk nearby and take copious notes of the patient's symptoms with a gold pen. Often she would interject to ask questions herself. Sometimes she would lead the conversation, pausing only to refer to her husband on certain points, which he seemed quite happy for her to do. The longest consultations would take about one and a half hours, but were usually much shorter in view of the sixty or more patients waiting outside. Hahnemann would often say to his patients that he would do his best for them but that 'God would have to give his blessing'. After the patients received their medicine, and usually a diet sheet, they were conducted downstairs to their carriages.

According to Melanie's own account, she assisted him in his work as his interpreter and secretary, making notes of the symptoms described by the patients and reminding him of the remedies in the *Materia Medica Pura* in which the symptoms were to be found. In this way, she claimed, he was able to see more patients before he became tired. Sometimes, by four in the afternoon more than one hundred poor patients would be waiting for treatment, and Hahnemann would allow her to treat many of them herself.

Hahnemann's policy on fees for his services had not changed throughout his career, since his days in Hettstedt. As far as possible he kept to the principle of 'no cure, no fee', and fees were calculated on a sliding scale according to the patient's means, whereby the very poor would pay nothing at all.

Since his arrival in Paris, Hahnemann had taken a new lease of life. After long, tiring days spent in his surgery, his evenings were crowded. The last of his poor patients would usually be seen about 6 p.m., after which he would have dinner. Most evenings he would visit his bedridden patients, travelling in his own carriage, accompanied by Melanie, or sometimes by one of his pupils.

Every Monday evening, between 8 and 10.30, local homoeopathic doctors, and those visiting Paris, would gather together in his home to discuss homoeopathic topics in a convivial atmosphere reminiscent of the social gatherings during his days in Leipzig. Seated in an armchair, wearing the now familiar smoking jacket and embroidered black velvet smoking cap with a black silk tassel (now in the museum in Hahnemann House in London), he would indulge in animated conversation. In spite of his advanced years, he had mastered fluent French. He still smoked his long pipe, which he sometimes waved as he spoke, to emphasize a point. He eschewed strong alcohol although he occasionally drank a little wine, brought to him on a silver salver by a liveried waiter.

Every other Thursday, he would attend either a concert, the Italian Opera, or the Théâtre Français, in the company of Melanie and her stepfather, M. Le Thiere. At least once a month, Melanie held a soirée in the grand salon, attended by the Paris socialites, with music and conversation sometimes into the early hours of the morning. Melanie always proved to be the perfect hostess at these events, and her winsome manner captivated everyone.

Melanie painted her husband's portrait several times, and one of these portraits (painted in 1838) was sent to his daughters in Köthen. Hahnemann also sat for several world-famous sculptors including David, Knolle, Woltreck and Staube (a bust of Hahnemann, sculptured by the celebrated David in 1835, is now located at Nelson's in London). Then, with what little spare time he had left, there were his letters to his family and his many friends.

Hahnemann summed up his feelings in a letter to his godfather, Baron von Gersdorff, written in June 1836:

> I am so happy in my present position as I never was before during the whole of my life. I have a highly educated wife who loves me dearly. . . . Her incessant care is only for me, even to the most trifling details, so that every wish of mine is fulfilled. This year we have not been separated for a single hour. . . . There cannot exist in

9. Bronze plaque of Hahnemann by David dated 1835, found in a
private collection in California in 1980.

Paris another couple which could equal us in perfect love. . . .
Acquaintances, who saw me years ago, assure me I look ten years
younger. This is the work of my precious Melanie, with whom I am
one in heart and soul, and who turns the evening of my life into an
earthly heaven.

Three months later he wrote in similar vein to Bönninghausen
in Münster, 'Even if I were fifty to sixty years younger, I would
never think of returning to Germany. . . . I am in better health
and happiness than I ever was in my life.' Clearly he had finally
found peace and an inner contentment, and Paris was now his
home.

Sometime between Hahnemann's departure for Paris and the
end of 1837, yet another of his tragic family met an untimely end.
His ninth child, Eleonore, was murdered in Köthen, where she
had returned after her divorce from Dr Wolff. Her nephew, Dr
Suss-Hahnemann, recalled some of the circumstances of her
death. Her body was found in a pond near Köthen, known as
Pheasants Pond. It is not known whether she was drowned or
whether she was dead on entering the water. It is known, however, that she had been seen in the company of a man on the day
of the murder. The man was arrested as a suspect and proved to be
a solicitor from Leipzig who had drawn up her Will only the day
before the murder, but he was released when he proved that he
had returned to Leipzig on the same day. Eleonore was buried in
the family vault at Köthen, but the murderer was never traced.

Of Hahnemann's ill-fated family, one was still-born; one son,
Ernst, had been killed whilst a baby and the other son, Friedrich
had deserted his family and suffered a mental breakdown; two of
his daughters, Frederika and Eleonore, had been murdered; two
daughters, Wilhelmina and Caroline, had died at an early age,
and three daughters had been divorced.

In view of his crowded life, it is not surprising that during his
entire stay in Paris, Hahnemann did not write a single book, nor
even an essay. In the summer of 1840, however, he began the
work on a thorough revision of the fifth edition of the *Organon*, of
which the last German edition had been published in 1833. 'I am
at work on the sixth edition of the *Organon*, he wrote in a letter to
Bönninghausen, 'to which I devote several hours a day on

Sundays and Thursdays, all other time being required for the treatment of patients who come to my rooms.' To his publisher in Düsseldorf, he wrote in a letter dated 20 February 1842, 'I have now, after eighteen months of work, finished my sixth edition of my *Organon*, the most nearly perfect of all.'

It was destined, however, not to be published until eighty years later. Melanie refused to part with the manuscript after Hahnemann's death and during her own lifetime, in spite of many lucrative offers, particularly from the homoeopathic doctors of America. The manuscript, which proved to be simply a carefully annotated copy of the fifth edition, written in Hahnemann's small, clear handwriting, was recovered eventually after it was nearly lost during the siege of Paris in the Franco-Prussian war of 1870-71 and again during the First World War.

Melanie's involvement in the medical side of her husband's practice caused mutterings amongst the medical establishments of Paris, who ultimately brought her before the courts for practising without medical qualifications. Anticipating such a move, Hahnemann wrote to Dr Hering in Philadelphia:

28 March 1841

I receive patients of all ranks even the highest, in our consulting room, and I only visit in my carriage, those who are confined to their beds. I do this chiefly in the evening, because I hold consultations from ten in the morning until four in the afternoon. . . . If I have been correctly informed, your Academy of Allentown grants diplomas to good homoeopaths. If that is so, you would confer a favour on me if you would send one to my dear wife, Melanie Hahnemann, *née* d'Hervilly, for she is better acquainted with homoeopathy, both theoretically and practically than any of my followers and she lives for our art.

The following year, Hahnemann wrote to Hering again, reminding him of his promise to grant the diploma and asking why Melanie had not yet received it. He even offered to send him a cheque to cover the expense, but in spite of his pleas, the diploma was never awarded, for reasons which were never entirely clear.

Hahnemann's correspondence over this period demonstrated that he was keenly interested in the development of homoeo-

10. Dr Constantine Hering.

pathy in Great Britain and America. Until his death, he corresponded regularly with his friends, Dr Hering in Philadelphia and Dr Quin in London. It will be recalled that when his old friend, Dr Stapf, visited him in Paris on his return from England, where he had treated Queen Adelaide, Hahnemann was most anxious to learn of the progress of homoeopathy there.

Notwithstanding their preference for allopathy, Hahnemann had a sneaking respect for the British medical profession, personified by William Harvey, William Cullen, Edward Jenner and John Brown. British homoeopathic doctors apart, he mentioned more than once that, in his opinion, Dr Stapf was playing a considerable part in popularizing homoeopathy in Britain. He also believed that he may have made some contribution himself. He wrote to Dr Stapf on 30 April 1838:

> Homoeopathy in France is very weak, although during the last six months there has been a livelier interest among the younger generation of physicians. In England, our system makes greater progress than in Paris, the successful cures I have achieved with English people, who have come here specially in order to receive homoeopathic treatment, may have contributed.

Among his British patients, whom he treated successfully, were the Marquis of Anglesey, whom he treated for the side-effects of a serious facial wound sustained at the Battle of Waterloo. Another particular case involved a poor, twelve-year-old boy from Scotland, named John Young, who had been seriously ill for two years and declared incurable. He was brought to Hahnemann by a benefactress and, after nine months free homoeopathic treatment, he was completely cured.

His interest in developments in England is shown by a letter Hahnemann wrote to Mr William Leaf. The letter, illustrated, reads as follows:

> My dear friend,
>   Perhaps the medicine I send you hereby will likewise do you some good, although it is a little softer. It is to be prepared and taken in the same manner, that is to say, in 36 tablespoonsful of water of what (after having shaken well the bottle every time) you

will take the first day a single tablespoonful and every day one more, thus the eighth day, eight. Then you so remain eight or ten days without taking any medicament and then you will relate to me the result.

I hope you will continue conscienciously the same regimen recommended by me as necessary for healing you—abstain utmost from pure wine, from coffee and from tea, and walk about every day in the open air.

I am very glad of the further establishment of our divine art in Great Britain. My wife presents to you and to Lady Leaf much compliments and I remain, Yours,

Samuel Hahnemann,
Paris, 29 March 1839

It was Mr Leaf, an influential supporter of homoeopathy, who was largely instrumental in persuading Hahnemann's daughter, Amalie, that her son, Leopold (Suss-Hahnemann), should study medicine. After Leopold had qualified in medicine in Leipzig, it was Mr Leaf who influenced his decision to settle in practice in London.

Amalie was the only daughter to visit her father during his life in Paris. Leaving Charlotte and Louise in their home in Köthen, where she had gone to live after the death of her second husband, she attended the sixtieth anniversary celebration of her father's doctorate on 10 August 1839. She wrote to her sisters, addressing them in the familiar family diminutives of 'Luischen' and 'Lottchen', to describe the happy event. The celebration generally followed the pattern of his jubilee ten years before in Köthen, but on this occasion Melanie's artistic influence was evident. The main drawing room of 1 Rue de Milan was adorned with flowers and was ablaze with the light of more than one hundred candles illuminating the portraits (including a lifesize portrait of Hahnemann painted by Melanie) on the walls.

When the distinguished guests were assembled, letters of congratulation from all over Europe were read, and the eighty-four year old Hahnemann was presented with a silver-gilt cup engraved 'For the Doctor's 60th Jubilee'. Then followed an evening of poems and music. The programme included recitals by the renowned pianist Clara Wieck (who married Hahnemann's fellow countryman, the composer Schumann, two years later) and the famous violinist, Max Böhrer. The festivities went on

11. Letter written to Mr William Leaf by Hahnemann, dated 29 March 1839.

until three in the morning of the following day. Hahnemann's only regret was that too few German doctors were present.

An honour conferred on Hahnemann on his eighty-sixth birthday gave him special pleasure. On 10 February, the City Council of his native Meissen unanimously approved the Freedom of the City to be awarded to their famous son, by which he became an 'honorary citizen' of the city for his distinguished services. The document was signed by the Mayor and presented to Hahnemann by the Saxon Ambassador in Paris. Hahnemann wrote to Meissen of his pleasure at the honour bestowed on him, and tendered his grateful thanks. He concluded:

> . . . All that I have hitherto done for the welfare of the noble race of man, I regard only as a duty and a debt. May God bless Meissen and her trusty citizens.

The present Mayor of Meissen has confirmed (1980) that Hahnemann's letter of thanks is still in their possession.

During his stay in Paris, Hahnemann's detractors whispered that he had become senile and unfit to practise. In December 1877 Hahnemann's last pupil, a Swiss doctor named H. V. Malan, who spent eighteen months with him in Paris in 1841-42, wrote a spirited denial of this accusation. 'I wish to state', he wrote, 'Dr Hahnemann's intellectual powers were not those of senility—far from it. I have seen him make many remarkable cures, heard him teach and speak with wonderful accuracy, learning and judgement, adorned with that deep modesty which was his remarkable attribute.'

But the old world that Hahnemann knew was changing rapidly. As he neared the end of his life, there was a dawning of a new era. The young Queen Victoria had ascended the throne in 1837 and, three years later, married Prince Albert of Saxe-Coburg-Gotha. Gladstone had already entered Parliament, and the penny post had been instituted. The work of the English steam pioneers Newcomen and Watt had, in 1830, led to the second phase of the Industrial Revolution. Stephenson had successfully applied the steam engine to a vehicle, and the 'Rocket' had pulled a single coach along part of the Liverpool to Manchester line. By the late 1830s railways were thrusting across

Europe. The early steamships of Bell in Scotland and Fulton in America were coming into regular seagoing service and the first submarines had been built. Hahnemann's life work, however, was not transitional, but enduring.

Hahnemann wrote to his daughters Charlotte and Louise, in Köthen, 'Take courage! Soon your wish to visit us in Paris may be fulfilled as railways are progressing everywhere in Germany, and are already extending to Frankfurt and in France up to the Rhine.' Their wish was never fulfilled, for not only were they too nervous to make the journey, but their dislike of Melanie caused them to hesitate. Moreover, the railway came to Köthen too late.

A few days after his eighty-eighth birthday, Hahnemann contracted bronchial catarrh. He had suffered from regular bouts during the spring for several years and at first he treated himself, but as his old and feeble condition deteriorated, he called in the help of another doctor. Knowing his life was drawing to its close, he spoke to Melanie, expressing the wish that the inscription on his grave should read *Non inutilis vixi* (I have not lived in vain). To Melanie's comment that, as he had relieved so many others and suffered so many hardships in his life Providence surely owed him some exemption from suffering, he is reported to have replied, 'To me, why to me? Everyone in this world works according to the gifts and powers which he has received from Providence. Providence owes me nothing. I owe much to Providence.'

Samuel Hahnemann died peacefully in his bed in the early hours of the morning of 2 July 1843. Later that day, Melanie called to the house Dr Georg Jahr, one of the few German homoeopathic doctors in Paris with whom Hahnemann had a close personal relationship. He found Melanie lying in tears by the body of her husband, whom he pronounced had been dead for five hours. Dr Jahr duly issued the death certificate.

A week before Hahnemann died, Amalie arrived in Paris accompanied by her seventeen year old son, Leopold, to see her father, but, according to Haehl (1922), she was not allowed to see him. Moreover, Melanie refused to allow several friends to visit him, in spite of their earnest appeals. Melanie's behaviour over the next few days was even more extraordinary. She received permission from the police to keep her husband's body in the house for up to fourteen days. She made no public announcement of his death and did not disclose the funeral arrangements, nor send out any invitations to attend. Samuel Hahnemann was buried in a public grave in Montmartre Cemetery on 11 July 1843.

Posterity will not dispute that Hahnemann was, at times, obdurate, intolerant and quarrelsome. Shortly after his return from his last visit to Leipzig, Hahnemann had written to Professor Hufeland to explain his philosophy:

> . . . But you, my dearest friend, imbued with the mild spirit that would attempt to unite everyone, bear with me—bear with the pure-minded seeker after truth, who is inflexible in his convictions, incorruptible by false doctrines and illusions, even though you may not take a bold look into the reddening dawn. . . .

Sir Henry Wotton may have had Hahnemann in mind in his lines:

> How happy is he born and taught
> That serveth not another's will
> Whose armour is his honest thought
> And simple truth his utmost skill.

At his death Hahnemann's long and bitter campaign for medical reform was already beginning to bear fruit. The old system of medical treatment, which he had charged as crude, barbaric, unhygienic and ineffective, was about to undergo a complete metamorphosis. The value of proper diet, regular exercise, adequate rest and improved sanitary conditions was slowly becoming an accepted part of medical practice. Although Broussais had died five years earlier, it would be more than fifty years before the last bastions of the practices of blood-letting and application of leeches would fall to enlightened opinion. Soon, compassion was to replace cruelty with the introduction of psychiatric treatment of mental illness. Hahnemann's theories were not transitional. Indeed, they were destined to become interwoven with the entire fabric of modern medical practice. The final irony is that his even greater work, enunciating the principles of homoeopathy, has overshadowed Samuel Hahnemann's undoubted contribution in other fields of medical progress.

EPILOGUE

From Germany, the practice of homoeopathy had spread throughout Europe, to the United States, to India and South America and to almost every country in the world. After Dr Quin introduced homoeopathy in Great Britain in the late 1830s, it had swept the country. Originally described as 'Homoeopathic Dispensaries', hospitals were established in all the major towns and cities, principally in Liverpool (1841), London (1849), Bristol (1852), Manchester (1860), Tunbridge Wells (1863) and Glasgow (1880). During an outbreak of cholera in 1854, only 16.4 per cent of patients treated at the London Homoeopathic Hospital (now the Royal London Homoeopathic Hospital) died, compared with a mortality in other hospitals of 51.8 per cent.

Leath and Ross were the first manufacturers of homoeopathic medicines in Great Britain. Leath began to publish homoeopathic literature in 1831 and was joined by Frederick Ross, a pharmacist, about 1855. They began to supply other pharmacies, which were springing up in large numbers, from addresses in Vere Street and St Paul's Churchyard, and the business finally closed during the Second World War.

Ernst Armbrecht was the son of Louis Armbrecht, who had established one of the earliest homoeopathic pharmacies in Germany. Ernst was born in 1834, and also qualified as a pharmacist in Hamburg in 1855. He travelled to London via Paris, and became a close friend of Dr Leopold Suss-Hahnemann, who was then practising in London. In 1860, he set up a homoeopathic pharmacy in London—Armbrecht Nelson & Comapny—preparing medicines according to the procedures laid down by Hahnemann. Ernst Armbrecht died in August 1912 and the business was carried on by his son, Ernst Nelson Armbrecht, who subsequently changed the name to A. Nelson & Co. Ltd. The pharmacy still flourishes today in Duke Street, where it had moved from its original home in St James in 1890. In recent years, modern laboratory and manufacturing facilities were established in South London and the company supplies homoeopathic medicines to pharmacies throughout the country.

Although Dr Hering was the principal architect of homoeo-pathy in the United States, it had been introduced into the country by a Danish doctor, Hans Gram, in the 1820's, when it quickly became popular. Homoeopathic treatment proved to be particularly successful with epidemic diseases, notably yellow fever, the traditional scourge of the southern States of America. By 1900, 20-25 per cent of all physicians in the United States practised homoeopathy, and there were 22 homoeopathic medical colleges and over 100 homoeopathic hospitals.

The first homoeopathic pharmacy was established in 1835, by William Boericke (Boericke & Tafel) in Philadelphia. In 1853, Dr Hermann Luyties set up a pharmacy in North Broadway, St Louis, Missouri, and this company, now known as Luyties Pharmacal Co., and located in Laclede Avenue, St Louis, still manufactures homoeopathic medicines today. Another company, Humphreys Pharmacal Inc., was formed a year later. The first homoeopathic pharmacy in California was established by Boericke and Runyon in San Francisco in 1870. The pharmacy was taken over in 1937 and re-named Mylans Pharmacy. In 1981, the pharmacy moved from O'Farrell Street, where it had been for fifty years, to Ellis Street. At the same time, it was re-named Nelson & Mylans Pharmacy to mark a new partnership with Nelsons of England.

It is estimated that, by the close of the nineteenth century, more than 400 million people were receiving homoeopathic treatment. Yet, in spite of the massive support for this intrinsically safe and effective therapy, it was still opposed by the medical establish-ment of the day.

At the International Congress of Homoeopathic Physicians held in 1896 a committee was elected for the re-interment of the

Founder of Homoeopathy and for the erection of a monument which would be worthy of him. In 1898 the authorities in Paris sanctioned the removal of the remains of Christian Frederick Samuel Hahnemann from his forlorn, neglected grave in the cemetery of Montmartre to the renowned cemetery of Père Lachaise.

At 8.30 p.m. on the 24 March 1898, the body was ceremoniously exhumed in the presence of representatives of the Central Homoeopathic Commission, the Gallic Homoeopathic Society, the Society of Homoeopathic Physicians of Rhineland and Westphalia, the British Homoeopathic Society (later the Faculty of Homoeopathy), the American Institute of Homoeopathy, and the Homoeopathic Medical Society of Belgium. Also attending the ceremony were laymen and representatives of the medical profession from Great Britain, the United States of America, France, Germany, Spain, Austria, Italy, Belgium, Holland, Brazil and Russia, together with the Police Commissioner of Paris and civic dignitaries, Dr Suss-Hahnemann and other members of the Hahnemann family and Mr Cloquemin, Vice-President of the Transatlantic Company, representing the Baroness of Bönninghausen.

The proceedings were opened by long speeches by Dr Cartier from Paris, the Secretary of the Committee, Dr Hughes from Brighton, Dr Suss-Hahnemann and Dr Leon Simon, who concluded his speech with the words:

> Hail Hahnemann! we bow before thy venerable remains, to which we, more fortunate than our predecessors, are able to render the honour due to them. Full of faith in the future, we appoint a meeting place before thy mausoleum for the physicians who shall be present at the International Congress of 1900. Thy tomb will appear the more beautiful to them illuminated by the dawn of the next century, which will see the triumph of thy doctrine.

The coffin was duly opened and the remains identified by a wedding ring, inscribed, *Samuel Hahnemann, Melanie de Hervilly. Verbunden, Köthen, 18 Janvier 1835*; the gold medal of the French homoeopaths and a letter from Melanie Hahnemann. A long plait of Melanie's hair was wound round his neck.

The procession then moved across Paris to the Père Lachaise

cemetery and there, with due pomp and ceremony and a speech of consecration by the Chairman of the International Committee, Dr Brasol of Petersburg, the remains of Samuel Hahnemann were lowered into their last resting place. 'The site of the new tomb is the most celebrated corner of this renowned cemetery,' reported the *Homoeopathic World* in July 1898:

> ... where all that France has achieved of greatness in science, fine art and war is represented. Music is represented by Rossini, Auber and Donizetti. Poets and famous writers are found there. Racine lies close to Hahnemann's side; a little further on Molière and Lafontaine. The sciences are represented by Gay-Lussac and Arago, and on the same side one sees the tombs of the Field Marshals Ney, Davout, etc. This is sufficient to show that the remains of this great and famous man have at last found a worthy resting place.

Two years later, on 21 July 1900, largely through the generosity of the homoeopathic doctors of America, and in the presence of representatives from many countries, a fitting monument was erected over the grave. The monument stands fourteen feet high, in polished Scottish granite, with a bust of Hahnemann and the inscription, *Hahnemann, Fondateur de L'Homoeopathie*, with his dates of birth and death. Later still, a secondary inscription was added:

Non inutilis vixi

The manner of his burial and reburial surely epitomized the dichotomy of Samuel Hahnemann's life. On one hand, rejection and contempt, and on the other, praise and veneration.

The old warrior had finally been laid to rest. But he had not lived in vain; others would now take up the homoeopathic banner and continue the fight, and even today the conflict continues. To meet self-interest, corruption, bigotry, prejudice and resistance to change is to know how Hahnemann felt. If homoeopathy is to play its true part in the relief of suffering, then its benefits should be made available to all the people, and not just the privileged few, for this is what Samuel Hahnemann would have wished.

BIBLIOGRAPHY

Albrecht, Franz. *Hahnemann Leben und Wirken.* Leipzig, 1875.

Ameke, W. *Origins and Fight for Homoeopathy.* 1884.

Barker, W. N. *Hahnemann the Pioneer.* London, 1922.

Bradford, T. L. *The Life and Letters of Dr Samuel Hahnemann:* Boericke & Tafel, Philadelphia, 1895.

British Homoeopathic Journal, The. Vol. LXIII, No. 4, p 217, 1974.

——, Vol. LXV, No. 1, p 48, 1976.

Brooke, John. *King George III:* Panther, 1972.

Coulter, Harris L. *Homoeopathic Influences:* Formur, 1973.

Creighton, Charles. *History of Epidemics in Britain.* Vol. I (1891), Vol. II (1894).

Dawson, W. H. *The Evolution of Modern Germany,* 1938.

——, *The Germany of the Eighteenth Century:* Educational Book Company, 1938.

Dudgeon, R. E. *Life and Work of Samuel Hahnemann,* 1854.

Fisher, H. A. L. *Napoleon Bonaparte.* 1913.

Fraser, Antonia. *The Lives of the Kings and Queens of England:* Futura, 1977.

Haehl, Richard. *Samuel Hahnemann, His Life and Work.* Leipzig, 1922.

Hahnemann, Samuel. *The Chronic Diseases, Their Peculair Nature and Their Homoeopathic Cure* (Translated by Prof. L. H. Tafel from the 2nd German edition of 1835): Boericke & Tafel, Philadelphia, 1896.

——, *Materia Medica Pura* Vols. I and II: Hahnemann Publishing Company, 1881.

——, *Organon of the Rational Art of Healing* (Translated by C. E.

Wheeler from the German edition of 1810): J. M. Dent, 1913.

——, *Organon of Medicine*, sixth edition (Translated by William Boericke): Boericke & Tafel, Philadelphia, 1952.

——, His own letters, originals, copies and translations.

Hamlyn, Edward. *The Healing Art of Homoeopathy: The Organon of Samuel Hahnemann*: Beaconsfield Publishers Limited, 1979.

Hobhouse, Rosa Waugh. *The Life of Christian Samuel Hahnemann*: C. W. Daniel, 1933.

Homoeopathic World, July 1898.

Humpert, Martin. *Hahnemann*: Fischer, 1945.

Knerr, Calvin B. *Life of Hering*: Magee Press, 1940.

Matthews, Leslie G. *History of Pharmacy in Britain*: Livingstone, 1962.

Mitchell, G. Ruthven. *Homoeopathy*: W. H. Allen, 1975.

Nelson, A. and Company Limited. London archives.

Norman, Sir George. *A Record of Medical Progress*: Educational Book Company, 1938.

Osler, Sir W. *The Evolution of Modern Medicine*. 1921.

Organon, The. Quarterly Journal of Homoeopathic Medicine, Vol. I, 1878.

Organon, The. Anglo-American Journal of Homoeopathy, No. 4, October 1878.

Partington, J. R. *Inorganic Chemistry*: Macmillan, London, 1946.

Royal London Homoeopathic Hospital, The. Centenary Brochure, 1949.

Shadman, Alonzo J. *Who is Your Doctor and Why?*: Keats, 1958.

Simon, Sir J. *English Sanitary Institutions*, second edition. 1897.

Singer, Charles. *A Short History of Medicine*: Oxford, 1928.

Stadt Archiv, Meissen.

Taine, H. A. *Les Origines de la France Contemporaine*, Vols I-VI. 1880.

Tyler, M. L. *Hahnemann's Conception of Chronic Disease as Caused by Parasitic Micro-organisms*: John Bale, 1933.

Weir, Sir John. *Hahnemann on Homoeopathic Philosophy*.

Zeller, Edward. *Geschichte der deutschen Philosophie seit Leibnitz*, second edition. 1875.

INDEX

-9. FEB. 1982